STECK-VAUGHN

Target SPELLING 780

TEACHER'S EDITION

Margaret Scarborough
Mary F. Brigham
Teresa A. Miller

STECK-VAUGHN
ELEMENTARY · SECONDARY · ADULT · LIBRARY
A Harcourt Company

www.steck-vaughn.com

ISBN 0-7398-2465-1

5 6 7 8 9   054   06 05 04 03

Contents

About the Authors

Margaret M. Scarborough teaches at Elizabeth Seawell Elementary School in Chapel Hill, North Carolina. Her master's degree was conferred by the University of North Carolina. Ms. Scarborough has taught kindergarten through sixth-grade students with special learning needs. She works collaboratively with regular classroom teachers, remedial reading teachers, speech and language pathologists, and behavioral therapists. She is a member of the Learning Disabilities Association of North Carolina and past president of the Orange County Association for Children and Adults with Learning Disabilities.

Mary F. Brigham is the principal of Bowley Elementary School in Fort Bragg, North Carolina. She has been a principal for ten years—four years at McNair Elementary School and six years at Bowley Elementary School. Ms. Brigham has led language arts, early childhood, and remedial reading programs for the Fort Bragg Schools, in addition to having had varied teaching experience at all levels. Ms. Brigham earned her master's degree at the University of North Carolina at Chapel Hill and completed a doctorate in Educational Administration in 1992 at Campbell University.

Teresa A. Miller has taught children in Virginia, Vermont, and North Carolina. Her degrees in education are from the College of William and Mary and the University of North Carolina at Chapel Hill. She works with both children and adults in a wide variety of educational settings.

Target Spelling is an alternative spelling program for students with special learning needs. The program was created by specialists in learning disabilities and remedial reading at Elizabeth Seawell Elementary School in Chapel Hill, North Carolina. The authors successfully used the program with their students before its publication. *Target Spelling* has since become a tried-and-true favorite of teachers. *Target Spelling* provides teachers with an excellent tool to use in guiding students in the strategies that good spellers use and in providing students with opportunities for practice.

This edition of *Target Spelling* retains the spelling strategies and features of the

original program that have repeatedly led students to spelling success, while adding several new features requested by teachers. Now with more opportunities for writing experiences, additional opportunities for review, even more focus on spelling strategies, a Word Study Plan, and standardized test practice pages, *Target Spelling* will maximize student learning.

> "Spelling is a complex language system with phonetic, semantic, historical, and visual demands."
> (Gentry & Gillet, *Teaching Kids to Spell*)

Each of the first three books—*Target 180, 360,* and *540*—present 180 words. The next three books—*Target 780, 1020,* and *1260*—each contain 240 words. The book titles are derived from the number of spelling words students have mastered as they complete each book successively.

To meet the needs of students with special needs, *Target Spelling* incorporates these features:

- A placement test to determine the proper entry level for each student
- A systematic method of study that provides a variety of stimulating and meaningful exercises—appropriate to a wide range of ages and abilities—to reinforce a positive attitude toward the study of spelling
- A limited number of spelling words introduced each week—six per week in *Target 180, 360,* and *540;* eight per week in *Target 780, 1020,* and *1260*
- A master word list for teachers to use in coordinating spelling instruction with the total language arts curriculum
- Instructional activities to accommodate a variety of learning modalities
- Relaxed pacing from lesson to lesson
- Clear, concise directions for each exercise
- Cloze paragraphs to test students' ability to use the spelling words in context
- Additional review pages every five lessons to reinforce student learning
- A checklist and a graph on which students can track their progress
- Standardized test practice pages to allow students to gain familiarity and comfort with test formats

Target Spelling is comprised of six worktexts based on the concept that the learning of spelling is a means to an end—to help students become better communicators—and not an end in itself. The aim of the program is to lead students to discover underlying linguistic patterns and relationships so that they can apply what they learn in *Target Spelling* to their other reading and writing experiences.

The lessons in *Target Spelling* follow a carefully designed instructional plan. The focus is on patterns and strategies, instead of spelling rules, to make the challenges of written communication easier for students with special needs. Words from a word family, such as "Words with -*ack*," are presented along with high-utility sight words to give students the quickest access to spelling the words they speak.

The first three books of *Target Spelling*— *180, 360,* and *540*—contain 162 of the 220 words from the Dolch Basic Sight Word List. The words on this list are "high frequency" words, or words that occur often in written and spoken language. The words in the next three books—*780, 1020,* and *1260*—include words with more complex linguistic patterns, commonly misspelled homonyms, phonemic patterns with prefixes and suffixes, and words of up to four syllables.

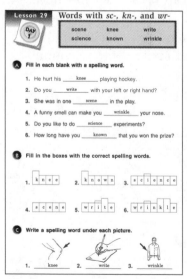

Each *Target Spelling* book is organized into thirty weeks of lessons, with four exercise pages per lesson. Lesson and day numbers are clearly indicated, and student pages are perforated to facilitate use. One exercise page is to be used each day for the first four days of the week (Days 1–4).

On the last day of the week (Day 5), teachers can administer the spelling test, using the dictation sentences provided on pages T13–T15. Students can write the spelling words on their own notebook paper.

My Word List at the back of each student book provides a place for students to record their weekly test results and to practice missed spelling words. A progress graph for recording weekly test scores is also provided. Review pages in the Pupil Edition and blackline master Review pages in the Teacher's Edition are available after every five lessons and can be used as alternate assessment tools or extra practice for students who need it. In addition, standardized test practice is available to help familiarize students with test formats.

New to this edition are features in the student book designed to provide more support for students with special needs.

- The *Word Study Plan* demonstrates a step-by-step method for learning to spell words.

- The *Spelling Strategies* page describes simple techniques that all good spellers use.

- *Review* pages after every five lessons help students review and maintain strategies, skills, and spelling patterns.

- The *Word Study Sheet* provides a framework for students as they read, spell, and write new words.

- *Graph Your Progress* encourages students to take ownership of their learning as they plot their spelling mastery from week to week.

"Children need to learn how to spell, not what to spell. They need generalizable strategies that can be applied in all spelling contexts."
(Rosencrans, *The Spelling Book*)

Target Spelling can be used flexibly to help meet the needs of students with spelling problems. The exercises are designed to be completed independently by students after each task has been introduced and explained by the teacher.

To facilitate learning and to allow students with special needs to implement spelling strategies, *Target Spelling* provides the following types of exercises:

- **Writing Practice** Many opportunities are provided for students to recognize and use spelling words in context. Prompts encourage students to write original sentences and, in the higher-level *Target Spelling* books, original paragraphs.

- **Cloze Paragraphs** This widely endorsed learning technique enables students to develop a broad range of vocabulary and reading skills.

- **Word Analysis** Students focus on elements of a word, examining similarities and differences among features of the spelling words. In this manner, students make their own generalizations about correct spelling.

- **Definition/Clue Exercises** Common meanings are reinforced and new meanings are taught. Students practice writing the spelling words.

- **Crossword Puzzles** This entertaining format guides students to understand the components of a word, its meaning, and its relationship to other words.

- **Review** To help students maintain and review strategies and skills, review pages are provided after every five lessons. The familiar formats of the pages foster student success.

- **Standardized Test Practice** To acquaint students with test formats, exercises are presented in formats students will encounter on standardized tests.

To further assist teachers, the following features are also included:

Placement Test This test helps teachers target words that students are unable to spell correctly. Teachers can test students before assigning specific *Target Spelling* books to them.

Dictation Sentences Sentences that use spelling words in context are provided to further enhance students' ability to understand and spell words in context. These sentences may be used when the weekly test is administered or as a reinforcement exercise. Spelling words from earlier *Target Spelling* lessons are often included to help students connect to previous learning.

Blackline Masters A variety of blackline masters are designed to be used flexibly to help teachers meet student learning needs. The *Word Study Sheet* describes the seven-step plan for student use in independent word study, and two assessment tools assist with record-keeping and documentation. The *Checklist for Informal Assessment* can be used to observe students' progress, and the *Student Progress Graph* may be used to graph the number of words a student spells correctly on his or her weekly test. In addition, review practice reinforces the content of the previous five lessons.

"Good spellers use different strategies to try words."
(Snowball & Bolton, *Spelling K–8*)

Determine Which Book to Use

Several tools can be used to determine which book is most appropriate for students. Teachers can consider students' approximate reading level, as well as use writing samples to evaluate spelling errors. The *Placement Test*, described on page T11, is designed to accurately gauge which *Target Spelling* book will be the most appropriate learning tool.

Introduce the Weekly Lesson

If using *Target 180*, teachers should read each word aloud and use it in a sentence. In other *Target Spelling* books, students can be involved in presenting the words. After the words are read aloud, guide students in a discussion about the words' meanings and about their relationship to one another.

Use the Exercises

A variety of exercises that utilize a multisensory approach involve students in learning and practicing the spelling words. As students first begin the exercises, teachers can explain and model the directions for the pages.  (See pages T7 and T8 for more specific examples of exercise formats.) As students become more familiar with the types of exercises, less modeling will be needed. When students understand the task, they can complete the pages independently. Then teachers can vary the method of evaluating the exercises. An answer key is provided for teachers to use when checking each exercise. Teachers may wish to involve students in checking their work as a group activity, or provide the answer key for students to use in self-checking.

Assess Student Learning

The *Dictation Sentences*, beginning on page T13, can be used to measure student mastery.  Mastery occurs when students miss no more than two spelling words. If students do not attain mastery, teachers can review and reteach. Encourage students to use *My Word List* to practice missed words. Teachers may also wish to use the dictation sentences as a pretest to help assess student needs.

Additional opportunities for assessment are presented in the student books as well as in the blackline masters in the Teacher's Edition:

- *Review* pages in both the Teacher's Edition and Pupil Edition can be used to check how well students are retaining mastery of five lessons.

- Standardized test format pages allow students to practice test-taking strategies while demonstrating mastery.

- *Graph Your Progress* presents an easy-to-use format for students to track their progress.

- The *Checklist for Informal Assessment* and the *Student Progress Graph* provide formats for observing and documenting skill growth.

"Assessment should be comprehensive and eclectic."
(Rosencrans, *The Spelling Book*)

The Exercises

The range of exercises in *Target Spelling* provides teachers with the opportunity to discover which approaches are most successful with individual students. The following exercises appear frequently in *Target Spelling* books. Their complexity and level of challenge increase as students move through the program. Throughout the exercises, students are given opportunities to practice and apply spelling strategies.

Recognition in Context

These activities reinforce learning of a word's meaning by requiring students to recognize the spelling word in context, or to supply the missing word in context.

A. Circle the spelling word. Then write it on the line.

1. (Can) you come to see me? __can__

B. Fill in each blank with the correct spelling word.

1. May I have __an__ apple?
    at   an

C. Fill in each blank with a spelling word.

1. You are my __best__ friend.

Cloze paragraphs are also frequently provided. Cloze paragraphs sharpen students' comprehension and strengthen their spelling skills. Teachers should direct students to read or listen to the entire passage before selecting the missing words. If students don't immediately recognize the appropriate word, suggest that they try each spelling word in the blank and reason through the choices. To modify this activity for auditory learners, record and play each cloze paragraph for students to use as they work the exercise.

Visual Discrimination

In these activities, students must be able to discriminate spelling words among words with similar letters. This format focuses students' attention on spelling patterns.

A. Circle the word that is the same as the top one.

rag	find	bag
raq	tind	bay
rab	fiud	dag
(rag)	(find)	beg
rap	finb	(bag)

B. Find the hidden spelling words.

```
e   l   e  (t   e   s   t)
s   o  (b   u   n   g   s
(a   r   e)(b   e   s   t)
s   e  (w   e   s   t)  u
t   r   o   n   t)  s   r
```

C. Put an *X* on the word that is <u>not</u> the same.

1. draw   draw   draw   darw✗   draw
2. plow   plow   plow   glow✗   plow
3. clown   clown   clawn✗   clown   clown
4. frown   frown   frown   frown   frowm✗

D. Circle each spelling word that is hidden in the big word. Write the word on the line.

1. (wag)on __wag__   2. b(rag) __rag__

Word Analysis

These activities require students to examine all facets of the spelling words, such as individual letters and word families so that they focus on elements of the words, as well as the word as a whole unit.

A. Find the missing letters. Then write the word.

1. p l a i n   plain
2. t r a i l   trail

B. Fill in the boxes with the correct spelling word.

1. rag   2. find   3. bag

C. Circle the letters that are the same in each spelling word.

peach   heat   clean   beans   read

D. Write the spelling word that rhymes with the word pair.

1. sing   thing   swing
2. pair   fair   hair

E. Write words that begin like each spelling word below.

whale	flake	snake
what	fly	snow

Crossword puzzles are another word analysis format used in *Target Spelling*.

Writing Practice

Students are directed to write spelling words accurately two or three times as a kinesthetic approach to learning the spelling words. The format of the exercise is designed to have students write the spelling words, rather than circling or underlining responses, to maximize the learning opportunities.

Creative Writing

Students apply what they have learned about spelling patterns and strategies in writing. Students may be asked to complete sentences, or write original sentences, using spelling words. In higher levels of *Target Spelling*, students are directed to write paragraphs.

A. Complete each sentence.

1. It's her turn to _____.
2. The fern I bought is _____.

Matching Words with Pictures

In these exercises, students practice recognizing visual cues and matching print to pictures by labeling illustrations with the correct spelling word.

Definition/Clue Exercises

These exercises reinforce meanings of spelling words in an entertaining and challenging way. Students draw conclusions to solve riddles or make associations, such as antonyms or synonyms.

A. Answer each question with a spelling word.

1. Which word is the same as two nickels?
   dime
2. Which word names a part of the body?
   spine

B. Write each spelling word beside its clue.

sea   1. the ocean
pail   2. a bucket

C. Write the spelling word that names things you can touch.

1. foot   2. book   3. wood

T8

Spelling Strategies

Throughout *Target Spelling*, students are encouraged to use spelling strategies to correctly spell words. Spelling strategies can help students notice word families and patterns among words, examine words visually to build a sense of what "looks right" in spelling, and think about the sounds of the words they are trying to spell. Spelling strategies create links between what students already know and new concepts.

• Strategies are described in easy-to-follow language on the *Spelling Strategies* page in the Pupil Edition. Simple tips that students can return to again and again are introduced.

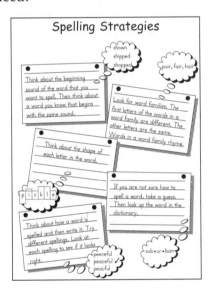

• The *Word Study Plan* in the Pupil Edition applies the strategies, giving students suggestions for things to try when spelling words.

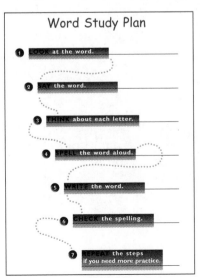

• The *Word Study Sheet* in the Pupil Edition guides students to apply the strategies as they work to spell the words. A blackline master of the *Word Study Sheet* is also provided in the Teacher's Edition.

Words	1 Look at the Word	2 Say the Word	3 Think About Each Letter	4 Spell the Word Aloud	5 Write the Word	6 Check the Spelling	7 Repeat Steps (if needed)

Word Study Sheet (Make a check mark after each step.)

Name _____

Guiding with Questions

Teachers can help students self-monitor and rely on strategies by prompting them with questions such as the following:

• What other word does this remind you of?

• Does it look right?

• What letters can stand for that sound?

• Close your eyes. Can you see the word?

• Is there a word part that you know?

• Do you recognize any word families?

• Can you find the word in the dictionary?

"Competent spellers use many strategies to try unfamiliar words and to learn words."
(Snowball & Bolton, *Spelling K–8*)

Activities for Various Learning Modalities

The authors of *Target Spelling* recognize that students learn in different ways. The program addresses three different learning styles: visual, auditory, and kinesthetic. Teachers can enhance student learning by presenting the following activities geared toward certain learning modalities.

Visual Learners

Write a short word, such as *an* on the board. One at a time, students add a letter to make a new word.

Have students change one letter of a spelling word to make new words.

Write spelling words on the board. Direct students to find smaller words within the word.

Have students illustrate spelling words and label the illustrations.

Draw a tic-tac-toe or crossword pattern and direct students to fill in words.

Write spelling words in one column on the board. Write words with a similar pattern in another column. Have students match words with close spellings.

Write any mnemonic devices, such as "The principal is your pal."

Kinesthetic Learners

Give each student in a small group one letter card of a spelling word. Have students arrange themselves in order to spell the word.

Label bags or boxes with word patterns. Give students word cards to sort according to pattern.

Write spelling words on the board. Have students use colored chalk to mark a spelling pattern in each word.

Have students type the spelling words or related words on a typewriter or computer keyboard.

Have teams of students act out the meaning of spelling words in a game of "Charades."

Have students trace spelling words cut from sandpaper letters.

Auditory Learners

Have students say and spell each word into a tape recorder, then play back the tape.

Write words on the board, circling a vowel, consonant, or pattern. Ask students to pronounce the sound the circled letters stand for, then name other words with that sound.

Recite a rhyme, short story, or series of sentences. Ask students to clap or make another signal when they hear spelling words.

Make letter cards with target sounds and word cards of the spelling words. Distribute the word cards to students. Hold up a sound card and have students hold up corresponding word cards and spell the word in unison.

The Placement Test

The Placement Test helps teachers target words that students are unable to spell correctly. Then students can be assigned an appropriate level of exercises.

Students should be tested individually, and only on the words within their instructional reading level. Teachers should call out the first word in a level, use the word in a sentence, and then repeat the word. It is recommended that when students miss three or more words at any level, this becomes the level at which they should be placed. The circled numbers to the left of each word group indicate instructional reading levels.

The following chart will aid teachers in placing students:

WORDS ON PLACEMENT TEST	NUMBER OF WORDS MISSED	BOOK INDICATED
1–10	Three or more	Target 180
11–20	Three or more	Target 360
21–30	Three or more	Target 540
31–40	Three or more	Target 780
41–50	Three or more	Target 1020
51–60	Three or more	Target 1260

1

TARGET 180

1. can	I can run very fast.	can
2. pen	Please help me put the pig in the pen.	pen
3. rack	I hung my coat on the rack.	rack
4. hill	Let's walk up that steep hill.	hill
5. pond	The ducks swim in the pond.	pond
6. nest	The birds built a nest in the tree.	nest
7. silk	Her new dress was made of silk.	silk
8. mitten	He lost one mitten while playing outside.	mitten
9. are	You are a good friend.	are
10. have	Have you been to see the circus?	have

2

TARGET 360

11. hurt	I fell down and hurt my knee.	hurt
12. what	What do you want to do today?	what
13. block	Have you ever seen a block of ice?	block
14. think	Do you think you can go?	think
15. trunk	An elephant has a trunk.	trunk
16. branch	The branch of the tree broke off.	branch
17. crash	Did you hear about the plane crash?	crash
18. shift	Do you have to shift gears in your car?	shift
19. spend	I can spend money very fast.	spend
20. strung	I strung the tree with lights.	strung

3

TARGET 540

21. location	Our house has a pretty location.	location
22. state	What state do you live in?	state
23. chair	Please sit in that chair.	chair
24. judge	Who was the judge in the court?	judge
25. spoil	If you leave the milk out, it will spoil.	spoil
26. bright	The sun is bright.	bright
27. frown	When I am sad, I have a frown on my face.	frown
28. wrinkle	Can you press the wrinkle out of my slacks?	wrinkle
29. caught	She caught the ball in her glove.	caught
30. toast	Toast and jelly taste good.	toast

4

TARGET 780

31. search	We will help you search for your lost dog.	search
32. launch	They will launch a rocket today.	launch
33. knew	He knew it was time to go home.	knew
34. thieves	The thieves were caught yesterday.	thieves
35. weren't	We weren't able to go skating.	weren't
36. wrench	She needed a wrench to fix her bike.	wrench
37. heal	Most cuts heal quickly.	heal
38. scratches	Our cat scratches those who tickle her.	scratches
39. freighter	The freighter sailed from New York to France.	freighter
40. illnesses	He has had both of those illnesses.	illnesses

5

TARGET 1020

41.	hoping	She was hoping it would snow today.	hoping
42.	slammed	The door slammed shut.	slammed
43.	heard	I heard a strange noise.	heard
44.	struggle	Did the animal struggle to get free?	struggle
45.	alphabet	The alphabet contains 26 letters.	alphabet
46.	scene	She painted a lovely scene of the ocean.	scene
47.	continue	He plans to continue the guitar lessons.	continue
48.	jewel	The jewel sparkles in the sun.	jewel
49.	personal	He had something personal to tell me.	personal
50.	vehicle	The vehicle we use most often is the truck.	vehicle

6

TARGET 1260

51.	thoughtful	My friend is thoughtful of others.	thoughtful
52.	you're	I hope you're planning to go with us.	you're
53.	uncertain	I am uncertain about this answer.	uncertain
54.	misfortune	He had the misfortune to lose his wallet.	misfortune
55.	collision	The collision of the cars occurred today.	collision
56.	believable	That story is not believable.	believable
57.	disconnect	Did he disconnect the telephone?	disconnect
58.	principal	The principal of our school is kind.	principal
59.	experience	She had a great camping experience last summer.	experience
60.	encouragement	With your encouragement, I will win the race.	encouragement

The following are sample placement test results that indicate placement for *Target 180*, *360*, and *540*. The placement tests for *Target 780*, *1020*, and *1260* should generally begin with word number 31.

This result indicates placement in *Target 180*.

1. can
2. pen
~~3.~~ reck (rack)
4. hill
~~5.~~ pant (pond)
~~6.~~ mess (nest)
~~7.~~ mik (silk)

STOP TEST

This result indicates placement in *Target 360*.

1. can
2. pen
3. rack
4. hill
5. pond
6. nest
7. silk
~~8.~~ miten (mitten)
9. are
10. have
11. hurt
12. what
~~13.~~ blok (block)
~~14.~~ thinck (think)
~~15.~~ truck (trunk)

STOP TEST

This result indicates placement in *Target 540*.

1. can
2. pen
3. rack
4. hill
5. pond
6. nest
7. silk
8. mitten
9. are
10. have
11. hurt
12. what
13. block
14. think
15. trunk
~~16.~~ brantch (branch)
17. crash
18. shift
19. spend
20. strung
21. location
~~22.~~ stat (state)
~~23.~~ chare (chair)
24. judge
25. spoil
~~26.~~ brihgt (bright)

STOP TEST

Dictation Sentences

Lesson 1

1. I like **her** very much.
2. I grew a **fern**.
3. Do not **jerk** the rope.
4. It takes **nerve** to fly.
5. A bird needs a **perch**.
6. A **verb** shows action.
7. I saw a **herd** of cattle.
8. The coffee will **perk**.

Lesson 2

1. The balloon **burst** very fast!
2. Please **turn** around.
3. The match will not **burn**.
4. A **nurse** took care of me.
5. The meeting is at the **church**.
6. The car sped around the **curve**.
7. I put the money in my **purse**.
8. I fell off the **curb**.

Lesson 3

1. They will **launch** the rocket.
2. **Gauze** is used in bandages.
3. The **vault** was empty.
4. Please **haul** the dirt away.
5. It is not my **fault**.
6. What is the **cause** of the fire?
7. A story said ghosts may **haunt**.
8. **August** is a hot month.

Lesson 4

1. I have a little **red** wagon.
2. I **read** the newspaper today.
3. You are **not** late.
4. Please tie a **knot** in the rope.
5. The **maid** cleaned our house.
6. He **made** his bed every day.
7. Will you **be** my partner?
8. A **bee** stung me.

Lesson 5

1. **Crawl** into the tunnel.
2. Our **lawn** gets mowed weekly.
3. We wake up at **dawn**.
4. It feels good to **yawn**.
5. A baby deer is called a **fawn**.
6. My cat's **claw** tore my coat.
7. A **flaw** is a mistake.
8. I wore a **straw** hat today.

Lesson 6

1. My **foot** was stuck in my shoe.
2. I put bait on the **hook**.
3. Their house has a **wood** stove.
4. I love to sit by the **brook**.
5. I **stood** up to speak.
6. The cat sat on the car's **hood**.
7. The shepherd's staff has a **crook**.
8. What food do you **cook**?

Lesson 7

1. Your **food** is cold.
2. **Noon** is a time of day.
3. When will the flowers **bloom**?
4. My tooth is **loose**.
5. The **booth** sells cotton candy.
6. I lost a **tooth** in the game.
7. I ran after the **goose**.
8. Do you have any **proof**?

Lesson 8

1. The **thief** ran away with the bag.
2. Are you the **chief** of this tribe?
3. I have a nephew and **niece**.
4. I ate a **piece** of pie.
5. We planted corn in the **field**.
6. **Shield** your eyes from the sun.
7. Speak loudly and be **brief**.
8. Slow down at the **yield** sign.

Lesson 9

1. The **road** is being paved.
2. She **rode** with me to school.
3. We filled the **pail** with sand.
4. You look sick and **pale**.
5. I **ate** too much turkey.
6. I drank **eight** glasses of water.
7. Did you **see** that man?
8. The ship went out to **sea**.

Lesson 10

1. Take a deep **breath**.
2. We **spread** the blanket on the ground.
3. Sew it up with **thread**.
4. Are you **ready** for this test?
5. You're as light as a **feather**.
6. I have on a **heavy** coat.
7. The **weather** will be sunny and cold.
8. I like your **leather** shoes.

Lesson 11

1. Have you **heard** that story?
2. When will we ever **learn**?
3. Did you **earn** that grade?
4. I have a **pearl** necklace.
5. The **earth** under our feet was soft.
6. Let's **search** for my watch.
7. I **yearn** to win the race.
8. I get up **early** every morning.

Lesson 12

1. Please don't **cry** over that.
2. Will you **fry** or bake the chicken?
3. **Dry** your hands.
4. She is a **shy** person.
5. Can you **fly** a kite?
6. The **sky** looks dark.
7. Don't **spy** on your friends.
8. Don't **pry** into his life.

Lesson 13

1. I like **to** go swimming.
2. I have **two** dollars.
3. I will vote **for** you.
4. He is **four** years old.
5. The **bear** was at the zoo.
6. The hilltop was **bare**.
7. Cakes are made with **flour**.
8. I will pick that **flower** for you.

Lesson 14

1. Have you ridden in a **sleigh**?
2. Put the **freight** on the truck.
3. How much do you **weigh**?
4. He gained **weight**.
5. You are a good **neighbor**.
6. Did you hear the horse **neigh**?
7. He lived to be **eighty** years old.
8. I saw the **freighter** at the dock.

Lesson 15

1. It hurts my knees to **kneel**.
2. Don't **knock** on the door.
3. The **knife** is sharp.
4. Do you know how to **knit**?
5. There's a **knot** in my hair.
6. The **knob** on the door fell off.
7. He was a king's **knight**.
8. A **knack** is something you do well.

Lesson 16

1. I need the **wrench** to fix the sink.
2. **Wring** out the wet cloth.
3. I hurt my **wrist**.
4. Hitting a person is **wrong**.
5. Was anyone hurt in the **wreck**?
6. I **wrestle** on the team at school.
7. The **wren** sat in her nest.
8. There's a **wreath** on the door.

Lesson 17

1. I **won't** be home for lunch.
2. We **aren't** going to the game.
3. It **isn't** my book.
4. **Doesn't** the dog have a home?
5. **Didn't** I see you at the show?
6. **Wasn't** that good food?
7. She **hasn't** been here.
8. We **weren't** going to buy that.

Lesson 18

1. The wind **blew** very hard.
2. Your eyes are **blue**.
3. I **hear** you very well.
4. Please stay **here** with me.
5. There's a **sale** at the store.
6. I put a new **sail** on my boat.
7. I **knew** him when we were boys.
8. I have a **new** coat.

Lesson 19

1. That's the last time **I'll** sing.
2. I think **you'll** win the contest.
3. **She'll** have to go.
4. If he's not careful, **he'll** hurt himself.
5. **I've** never been to the island.
6. **You've** got what it takes.
7. **We've** got to get out of this place.
8. **They've** got a lot of money.

Lesson 20

1. How many **bushes** did you plant?
2. I can grant you three **wishes**.
3. The machine **crushes** the cans.
4. The light **flashes** in my eyes.
5. She **brushes** her hair every night.
6. She washed all the **dishes**.
7. My dad **washes** the car once a week.
8. She **fishes** with a bamboo pole.

Lesson 21

1. They make **boxes** at that store.
2. I just read a book about **foxes**.
3. My mom **fixes** our TV.
4. My sister **waxes** her car.
5. We just paid our **taxes**.
6. They need many **axes** to cut down trees.
7. This part always **mixes** me up.
8. He rolled two **sixes** on the dice.

Lesson 22

1. Birds perch on tree **branches**.
2. She makes great **speeches**.
3. My **stitches** come out today.
4. There are **scratches** on my car.
5. All **churches** in our town ring bells.
6. He always **catches** a cold in winter.
7. I don't need my **crutches** anymore.
8. Your dress **matches** your shoes.

Lesson 23

1. She saves **pennies** in her bank.
2. The **babies** are asleep.
3. **Cherries** grow on that tree.
4. We picked **berries** on the farm.
5. They train **ponies** for the circus.
6. The dog had six **puppies**.
7. I have lived in many **cities**.
8. We need new **guppies** for our fish tank.

Lesson 24

1. A **hare** looks like a rabbit.
2. Don't pull my **hair**.
3. My cat has no **tail**.
4. A **tale** is a story.
5. Please **sew** this button on for me.
6. When will we **sow** the seeds?
7. A cut takes a while to **heal**.
8. Gum is stuck to the **heel** of my shoe.

Lesson 25

1. We raked the **leaves**.
2. I hear the **wolves** howl at night.
3. **Knives** and forks go together.
4. The mother cow fed her **calves**.
5. I put the food on the **shelves**.
6. The **thieves** stole my radio.
7. I baked **loaves** of bread.
8. Does a cat have nine **lives**?

Lesson 26

1. The women wore colorful **dresses**.
2. The **bosses** are in a meeting.
3. This book tells about **illnesses**.
4. I went to all my **classes**.
5. We washed all the **glasses**.
6. You get three **guesses**.
7. The boy **kisses** the girl in the story.
8. The coach had more wins than **losses**.

Lesson 27

1. All the **men** played soccer.
2. There are ten **women** in my class.
3. **Children** are invited to the play.
4. I brush my **teeth** twice a day.
5. I keep **mice** for pets.
6. The cart was pulled by a team of **oxen**.
7. **Sheep** give us wool for our clothes.
8. A flock of **geese** flew south today.

Lesson 28

1. I **know** how to read and write.
2. **No** one knows that she is here.
3. Can you **write** me a letter?
4. I can't find my **right** shoe.
5. I will be there in an **hour**.
6. **Our** son is a great kid.
7. My **son** and I are friends.
8. The **sun** is a bright star.

Lesson 29

1. I'll take **anyone** who wants to go.
2. Do you want **anything**?
3. Do you know **anybody** here?
4. I will go **anyplace** with you.
5. I didn't want dessert, **anyhow**.
6. **Anywhere** you go, I'll follow.
7. It's late, but we'll go **anyway**.
8. I'll be here **anytime** you need me.

Lesson 30

1. **Someone** is ringing the doorbell.
2. Is **something** making you sad?
3. I know **somebody** like that.
4. Let's go **someplace** for lunch.
5. **Somehow** I got lost.
6. I've seen him **somewhere** before.
7. Please take me to see her **sometime**.
8. I'd like to go there **someday**.

Master Word List

The following spelling words presented in *Target Spelling* are listed in alphabetical order by book. The number after each word identifies the lesson in which the word is taught. See pages 135–140 in each student book for a lesson-by-lesson word list.

Target 180

a–1	brim–29	fast–17	lamp–12	new–24	rust–19	tent–16
all–17	bring–28	felt–21	land–14	no–26	sack–6	test–18
am–17	bump–13	fill–9	last–17	not–9	sad–2	that–28
an–1	but–20	find–3	lend–15	now–26	said–11	they–29
any–30	butter–20	fist–19	less–11	on–21	sand–14	this–29
are–18	came–11	flick–27	like–23	one–9	see–11	three–13
as–1	camp–12	fling–28	list–19	our–24	sell–8	tick–7
ask–23	can–1	fond–25	little–6	out–24	send–15	to–16
at–1	cast–17	for–14	lock–10	pack–6	sent–16	trap–26
ate–20	clap–26	funny–3	look–7	pen–4	she–27	trim–29
away–1	click–27	get–22	lump–13	pet–5	sick–7	two–13
bad–2	cling–28	go–14	mad–2	pick–7	silk–22	up–16
bag–3	come–2	good–22	make–7	pill–9	skim–29	wag–3
band–14	crop–30	hand–14	mask–23	play–10	slap–26	was–30
batter–20	dad–2	have–21	mast–17	please–25	slick–27	we–12
be–18	damp–12	he–4	me–8	pond–25	slim–29	well–8
bell–8	dent–16	help–5	melt–21	prop–30	so–27	went–16
belt–21	did–23	hen–4	mend–15	pump–13	sock–10	west–18
bend–15	do–23	here–5	mess–11	rack–6	soon–28	wet–5
best–18	dock–10	hill–9	milk–22	rag–3	sting–28	where–15
better–20	down–2	ill–9	mist–19	ramp–12	stop–30	wrap–26
big–4	drop–30	into–22	mitten–24	ran–25	tack–6	written–24
bitter–20	dump–13	jet–5	must–19	red–10	tag–3	yellow–15
blue–4	dust–19	jump–6	my–8	ride–25	task–23	you–12
bond–25	eat–21	kick–7	nest–18	rock–10	tell–8	
brick–27	elk–22	kitten–24	net–5	run–11	ten–4	

Target 360

about–16	cash–28	flash–28	lunch–28	scalp–4	spill–6	trust–11
after–11	champ–26	flesh–29	many–2	scan–4	stamp–6	try–3
again–11	chat–26	flip–2	melon–20	scrap–4	strap–10	twenty–27
always–29	check–26	flute–5	mind–20	scrub–4	string–10	twin–27
arm–7	chest–26	four–7	much–8	seldom–17	strung–13	under–22
bank–12	class–11	fresh–29	myself–8	seven–22	studied–21	use–17
basket–16	club–11	frog–9	never–6	shack–23	studies–21	visit–16
because–29	collar–14	full–14	off–21	shall–23	study–6	visitor–17
been–19	crack–8	glad–2	petal–19	shelf–23	swim–7	want–23
before–19	crash–8	glass–2	picnic–18	shell–23	swimming–7	warm–6
black–1	crush–30	goes–5	pinch–12	shift–24	swing–7	wash–2
blanket–16	crust–8	grab–9	plant–3	ship–24	swung–13	were–30
bled–1	cupful–22	grass–9	plenty–4	shock–24	table–30	what–25
blend–1	dish–29	group–10	plus–3	shop–24	thank–15	when–25
blink–14	doctor–17	handful–22	press–10	shut–25	their–18	which–25
block–1	does–24	hang–28	pretty–15	signal–19	there–20	white–25
book–7	dollar–14	happily–20	prompt–10	skate–21	these–15	who–27
both–24	done–9	helpful–22	quick–27	skill–5	think–15	will–27
bottle–19	drank–12	hive–16	quit–27	skin–21	those–15	wink–14
bottom–17	drink–9	hurt–14	rabbit–16	skunk–5	thunder–25	wish–29
branch–13	drum–9	hush–30	ranch–13	slept–3	today–13	with–26
brown–4	eight–15	inch–12	rush–30	slid–3	together–13	woman–1
brush–30	empty–18	junk–12	sadly–20	small–3	too–22	wonder–1
bunch–28	fifty–18	kind–8	sang–28	snack–5	traffic–18	yes–26
candle–19	first–23	laugh–10	saw–17	snap–5	trip–11	
carry–21	flag–2	lemon–20	say–18	spend–6	trunk–12	

Target 540

age–27	base–11	beard–30	bite–15	boat–9	brain–7	bright–27
arrow–21	beak–6	bee–1	blade–10	bore–22	brave–12	broke–16
art–20	beans–2	bike–13	board–30	born–22	bread–24	broom–8

(continued on next page)

Target 540 *continued*

brought–28
cage–27
cane–11
care–19
case–11
caught–28
chair–19
chance–26
chew–24
clean–2
clear–21
cloud–5
clown–3
coast–9
code–16
coin–4
cold–18
cool–8
could–30
dance–26
dark–20
deal–6
deer–21
dime–14
dirt–30
don't–18
draw–3
dream–6
drew–24
drive–15
drove–17
due–24
edge–26
every–30
face–25
fair–19
far–20
feet–1
flake–10
flame–12
floss–23
free–1
frown–3
fudge–26
give–2
glide–13
grape–11
grime–14
groom–8
ground–5
head–24
hear–21
heat–2
hedge–26
high–27
hold–18
home–16
how–3
ice–25
join–4
joke–16
joy–4
judge–26
knee–29
know–16
known–29
law–3
leap–6
life–13
light–27
live–23
load–9
location–25
long–23
mail–7
meet–1
mile–14
moon–8
narrow–21
note–17
oil–4
once–1
only–23
own–18
paid–7
pane–11
pave–12
peach–2
plain–7
plate–12
plow–3
pole–17
pound–5
price–25
pride–13
proud–5
read–2
real–6
ripe–15
road–9
rode–16
rose–17
scale–10
scar–20
scene–29
science–29
scout–5
scrape–11
shade–10
share–19
shark–20
sigh–27
skirt–30
slope–17
snake–10
snore–22
snow–18
space–25
spare–19
speak–6
spine–14
spoil–4
spoon–8
stare–19
start–20
state–12
station–25
steer–21
stone–17
strike–13
stripe–15
strong–23
tame–12
taught–28
though–28
thought–28
throat–9
through–28
throw–18
toast–9
tool–8
toss–23
toy–4
trail–7
trout–5
value–24
vine–14
wait–7
whale–10
while–14
why–15
wife–13
wise–15
world–22
worn–22
worth–22
wrinkle–29
write–29
your–1

Target 780

anybody–29
anyhow–29
anyone–29
anyplace–29
anything–29
anytime–29
anyway–29
anywhere–29
aren't–17
ate–9
August–3
axes–21
babies–23
bare–13
be–4
bear–13
bee–4
berries–23
blew–18
bloom–7
blue–18
booth–7
bosses–26
boxes–21
branches–22
breath–10
brief–8
brook–6
brushes–20
burn–2
burst–2
bushes–20
calves–25
catches–22
cause–3
cherries–23
chief–8
children–27
church–2
churches–22
cities–23
classes–26
claw–5
cook–6
crawl–5
crook–6
crushes–20
crutches–22
cry–12
curb–2
curve–2
dawn–5
didn't–17
dishes–20
doesn't–17
dresses–26
dry–12
early–11
earn–11
earth–11
eight–9
eighty–14
fault–3
fawn–5
feather–10
fern–1
field–8
fishes–20
fixes–21
flashes–20
flaw–5
flour–13
flower–13
fly–12
food–7
foot–6
for–13
four–13
foxes–21
freight–14
freighter–14
fry–12
gauze–3
geese–27
glasses–26
goose–7
guesses–26
guppies–23
hair–24
hare–24
hasn't–17
haul–3
haunt–3
heal–24
hear–18
heard–11
heavy–10
heel–24
he'll–19
her–1
herd–1
here–18
hood–6
hook–6
hour–28
I'll–19
illnesses–26
isn't–17
I've–19
jerk–1
kisses–26
knack–15
kneel–15
knew–18
knife–15
knight–15
knit–15
knives–25
knob–15
knock–15
knot–4
knot–15
know–28
launch–3
lawn–5
learn–11
leather–10
leaves–25
lives–25
loaves–25
loose–7
losses–26
made–4
maid–4
matches–22
men–27
mice–27
mixes–21
neigh–14
neighbor–14
nerve–1
new–18
niece–8
no–28
noon–7
not–4
nurse–2
our–28
oxen–27
pail–9
pale–9
pearl–11
pennies–23
perch–1
perk–1
piece–8
ponies–23
proof–7
pry–12
puppies–23
purse–2
read–4
ready–10
red–4
right–28
road–9
rode–9
sail–18
sale–18
scratches–22
sea–9
search–11
see–9
sew–24
sheep–27
she'll–19
shelves–25
shield–8
shy–12
sixes–21
sky–12
sleigh–14
somebody–30
someday–30
somehow–30
someone–30
someplace–30
something–30
sometime–30
somewhere–30
son–28
sow–24
speeches–22
spread–10
spy–12
stitches–22
stood–6
straw–5
sun–28
tail–24
tale–24
taxes–21
teeth–27
they've–19
thief–8
thieves–25
thread–10
to–13
tooth–7
turn–2
two–13
vault–3
verb–1
washes–20
wasn't–17
waxes–21
weather–10
weigh–14
weight–14
weren't–17
we've–19
wishes–20
wolves–25
women–27
won't–17
wood–6
wreath–16
wreck–16
wren–16
wrench–16
wrestle–16
wring–16
wrist–16
write–28
wrong–16
yawn–5
yearn–11
yield–8
you'll–19
you've–19

Target 1020

able–26
above–1
afraid–1
agree–1
alone–1
alphabet–13
amaze–1
ankle–25
another–3
apple–21
argue–18
around–1
avenue–18
avoid–1
awake–1
barrel–20
battle–24
beat–29
beet–29
beetle–24
bicycle–28
biting–5
bother–3
brake–23
break–23
brightest–15
brother–3
buckle–25
bugle–27
bushel–20
buy–8
by–8
cable–21
canned–11
canning–6

(continued on next page)

Target 1020 *continued*

chapter–16
chased–10
cheaper–14
chimney–30
chopper–9
chuckle–25
cleanest–15
clever–16
clipper–9
closed–10
closet–2
clue–18
coming–5
continue–18
corner–16
cover–16
cradle–22
crinkle–25
cruel–20
dear–17
deer–17
dew–4
dial–19
diner–7
do–4
drizzle–28
dropped–11
dropper–9
dropping–6
duel–20

editorial–19
either–3
elephant–13
enter–16
example–28
fable–26
farther–3
father–3
fickle–25
filed–10
formal–19
fresher–14
fuel–20
fumble–26
gargle–27
gentle–24
geography–13
giggle–27
giver–7
glider–7
glue–18
gripping–6
handle–22
having–5
heard–12
herd–12
hiked–10
hockey–30
hole–8

hoping–5
hopped–11
hopping–6
humble–26
humming–6
jacket–2
jersey–30
jewel–20
jingle–27
jogger–9
journey–30
juggle–27
jungle–27
kettle–24
knight–4
knows–12
lead–23
led–23
living–5
loving–5
mail–8
making–5
male–8
maple–21
marble–26
market–2
meat–17
meet–17
metal–19
middle–22

monkey–30
mother–3
moved–10
mumble–26
neatest–15
needle–22
nephew–13
night–4
normal–19
nose–12
nozzle–28
older–14
one–17
other–3
pain–23
pane–23
pedal–19
peddle–22
people–21
personal–19
photo–13
phrase–13
pickle–25
pinning–6
pocket–2
poodle–22
poorest–15
pore–17
pour–17
pulley–30

purple–21
quicker–14
quickest–15
racket–2
rap–8
rattle–24
rescue–18
riddle–22
rifle–28
ripped–11
rocket–2
ruler–7
saddle–22
sample–28
scene–29
scraped–10
scrubbed–11
seen–29
settle–24
sharpest–15
shaver–7
shipped–11
shipping–6
shopper–9
sight–4
silver–16
simple–21
single–27
site–4
skater–7

slammed–11
slipper–9
smaller–14
smarter–14
socket–2
softest–15
sphere–13
stable–26
staple–21
statue–18
steal–29
steel–29
steeple–21
stepped–11
stopping–6
stronger–14
struggle–27
tackle–25
tattle–24
telephone–13
thicker–14
thimble–26
ticket–2
tickle–25
timed–10
title–24
towel–20
trial–19
true–18
turkey–30

used–10
using–5
valley–30
vehicle–28
voter–7
vowel–20
wade–4
waffle–28
wander–16
warmest–15
weak–29
wear–12
weather–12
week–29
weighed–4
where–12
whether–12
whisper–16
whole–8
winner–9
wiper–7
won–17
wood–23
would–23
wrap–8
zipper–9

Target 1260

admission–25
admittance–28
advertisement–18
affection–23
air–19
allowed–30
aloud–30
ambulance–28
apology–29
appearance–28
argument–18
attendance–28
audible–20
base–19
bass–19
beautiful–14
believable–21
biology–29
blackness–15
bough–4
bow–4
bravely–17
breakable–21
careful–14
careless–13
caution–23
coarse–26
coincidence–27
coldness–15
collision–24
company–29
competence–27

comprehension–25
concern–10
concert–10
conduct–10
conference–27
confide–10
confidence–27
conform–10
confusion–24
congregate–10
consent–10
construction–23
contract–10
correctly–17
country–29
course–26
darkness–15
decide–11
decision–24
decrease–11
deflate–11
dehydrate–11
deliver–11
depart–11
deposit–11
descend–11
difference–27
direction–23
disagree–5
disappear–5
disconnect–5
discount–5
dishonest–5
disinfect–5

dislike–5
disorganize–5
doe–19
dough–19
edible–20
education–23
encouragement–18
endurance–28
enemy–29
enjoyment–18
entrance–28
equipment–18
erosion–24
expansion–25
experience–27
explosion–24
extension–25
factory–29
fair–12
fairness–15
fare–12
finance–28
flea–26
flee–26
forth–16
fourth–16
friendly–17
guessed–30
guest–30
hall–8
harmful–14
harmless–13
haul–8
heir–19
helpless–13

honestly–17
hopeful–14
hopeless–13
horrible–20
idle–26
idol–26
incredible–20
independence–27
invasion–24
it's–12
its–12
kindness–15
library–29
likable–21
loudness–15
lovable–21
misbehave–9
misfortune–9
mislead–9
misplace–9
misprint–9
mission–25
mistreat–9
misunderstand–9
misuse–9
movable–21
mystery–29
nonbreakable–2
nonfat–2
nonfiction–2
nonliving–2
nonsense–2
nonsmoking–2

nonstick–2
nonstop–2
operation–23
painless–13
pair–8
partly–17
passed–16
past–16
patience–22
patients–22
payment–18
peace–4
peaceful–14
pear–8
peer–19
performance–28
permission–25
piece–4
pier–19
plain–16
plane–16
possession–25
possible–20
precook–3
preheat–3
prepaid–3
prepare–3
preschool–3
presence–30
presents–30
pretest–3
prevent–3
preview–3
principal–30
principle–30

protection–23
quickly–17
quietly–17
rain–8
recharge–7
reclaim–7
recycle–7
refill–7
refund–7
rein–8
repair–7
retirement–18
returnable–21
review–7
rewind–7
safely–17
sensible–20
shone–12
shown–12
sickness–15
slowness–15
some–4
stake–16
statement–18
steak–16
subfreezing–6
submarine–6
submerge–6
subsoil–6
subtitle–6
suburban–6
subway–6
subzero–6
sum–4
television–24
tension—25

terrible–20
thankful–14
thankless–13
their–8
there–8
thoughtful–14
thoughtless–13
threw–22
throne–12
through–22
thrown–12
transportation–23
truthful–14
unaware–1
uncertain–1
unequal–1
unhappy–1
unhealthy–1
unjust–1
unlikely–1
unsafe–1
usable–21
useless–13
vain–26
valuable–21
vein–26
violence–27
visible–20
vision–24
waist–4
waste–4
who's–22
whose–22
your–22
you're–22

Program Scope and Sequence

	Syllables/ Sight Words	Consonants/ Vowels	Word Meaning/ Usage	Word Analysis
TARGET 180 Reading Level: 1–2	• one-syllable words • sight words	• consonants and short vowels • consonant blends with short vowels • consonant digraphs • silent-letter combinations	• context clues	
TARGET 360 Reading Level: 2–3	• one-syllable words • two-syllable words • sight words	• consonants and short vowels • consonant blends with short vowels • consonant digraphs • silent-letter combinations	• context clues	
TARGET 540 Reading Level: 3	• one-and two-syllable words • three-syllable words • sight words	• consonants and long vowels • consonant blends with long vowels • consonant and vowel digraphs • diphthongs • silent-letter combinations	• context clues	
TARGET 780 Reading Level: 4	• one-and two-syllable words • three-syllable words	• consonant blends • consonant and vowel digraphs • diphthongs • silent-letter combinations • words with r-controlled vowels	• homonyms • context clues	• compound words • contractions • plurals
TARGET 1020 Reading Level: 5	• one-and two-syllable words • three-syllable words • four-syllable words	• consonant blends • consonant and vowel digraphs • diphthongs • silent-letter combinations	• homonyms • comparative/ superlative adjectives • context clues	• words with inflectional endings • words with -er as action agent
TARGET 1260 Reading Level: 6	• one- and two-syllable words • three-syllable words • four-syllable words	• consonant blends • consonant and vowel digraphs • diphthongs • silent-letter combinations	• homonyms • context clues	• compound words • words with inflectional endings • prefixes • suffixes

Word Study Sheet

(Make a check mark after each step.)

Words	1 Look at the Word	2 Say the Word	3 Think About Each Letter	4 Spell the Word Aloud	5 Write the Word	6 Check the Spelling	7 Repeat Steps (if needed)

Name _____

Checklist for Informal Assessment

Student's Name _____

Spelling Behaviors	Comments	Date
Readily attempts to spell new words		
Relies on a variety of strategies to spell new words		
Explains use of spelling strategies		
Recognizes and applies spelling patterns and word families		
Recognizes rhyming words		
Uses sound-symbol relationships to spell words		
Demonstrates understanding of segmenting words		
Uses inflectional endings		
Understands contractions		
Forms plurals		
Understands compound words		
Identifies homonyms		
Recognizes comparatives and superlatives		
Uses prefixes and suffixes		
Spells previously introduced high-frequency words correctly		
Understands meanings of spelling words		
Uses spelling words correctly in context		
Uses the dictionary		
Locates spelling errors in writing		
Corrects spelling errors in writing		
Maintains and refers to *My Word List*		
Consistently completes assigned spelling exercises		
Shows positive attitude toward spelling		
Explains why spelling is important		

Student Progress Graph

Number of words spelled correctly:

(After each weekly test, you may wish to graph the number of words a student spells correctly.)

Number of words spelled correctly:	Lesson 1	Lesson 2	Lesson 3	Lesson 4	Lesson 5	Lesson 6	Lesson 7	Lesson 8	Lesson 9	Lesson 10	Lesson 11	Lesson 12	Lesson 13	Lesson 14	Lesson 15	Lesson 16	Lesson 17	Lesson 18	Lesson 19	Lesson 20	Lesson 21	Lesson 22	Lesson 23	Lesson 24	Lesson 25	Lesson 26	Lesson 27	Lesson 28	Lesson 29	Lesson 30
8																														
7																														
6																														
5																														
4																														
3																														
2																														
1																														

Name _____

T22

Review for Lessons 1–5

T25
A. 1. burn, fern, turn   2. jerk
3. purse   4. curve
5. haul, crawl   6. cause
B. 1. August   2. fawn   3. crawl
C. turn, dawn, crawl, yawn, be

T26

D. Across	Down
1. verb	2. bee
3. perch	4. her
5. fault	5. fern
6. purse	7. red
8. burn	8. burst
9. herd	10. read
12. turn	11. knot
13. lawn	

Test Practice for Lessons 1–5

T27	**T28**
A.	**B.**
Example: B) dad	Example: A) friend
1. B) perch	1. D) read
2. D) curve	2. A) made
3. C) vault	3. B) fault
4. B) fern	4. A) straw
5. A) purse	5. C) knot
6. C) perk	6. D) dawn
7. A) burn	7. A) crawl
8. B) haul	8. C) cause
9. D) herd	9. C) lawn

Review for Lessons 6–10

T29
A. 1. brook, hook   2. bloom   3. field
4. eight, ate   5. pail, pale
B. noon
C. wood, pail, cook, field

T30

D. Across	Down
1. tooth	2. hood
3. foot	3. food
5. wood	4. thief
8. eight	6. shield
9. road	7. breath
11. field	10. weather
12. thread	
13. yield	

Test Practice for Lessons 6–10

T31	**T32**
A.	**B.**
Example: D) letter	Example: C) bridge
1. B) foot	1. C) shield
2. A) tooth	2. B) rode
3. D) piece	3. C) eight
4. B) goose	4. D) heavy
5. A) proof	5. A) thread
6. C) loose	6. D) ready
7. B) noon	7. C) leather
8. D) booth	8. A) field
9. C) chief	9. A) ate

Review for Lessons 11–15

T33
A. 1. fry, shy, fly   4. knock
     sky, spy, pry   5. to, two
2. flour, flower
3. sleigh, neigh, weigh
B. 1. freight, weight, knight
2. two, flower, weigh, weight
C. early, sky, two, fly, neighbor, to

T34

D. Across	Down
2. sleigh	1. flower
3. knob	3. knife
5. yearn	4. eighty
7. neigh	6. knack
8. cry	10. kneel
9. sky	11. early
11. earth	
12. neighbor	
13. learn	

Test Practice for Lessons 11–15

T35	**T36**
A.	**B.**
Example: C) knit	Example: B) joke
1. D) heard	1. C) eighty
2. C) fry	2. C) knob
3. B) four	3. A) knife
4. A) earn	4. D) weigh
5. C) shy	5. B) neighbor
6. D) search	6. C) sleigh
7. A) early	7. A) knock
8. B) cry	8. C) freight
9. D) sky	9. D) knack

Review for Lessons 16–20

T37
A. 1. wrench   2. blew, blue, knew, new

3. wishes   4. hear, here

5. brushes   6. flashes

B. wishes, They've, I'll

C. 1. won't   2. he'll   3. isn't   4. you'll

5. didn't   6. they've   7. doesn't

T38

D. Across	Down
1. knew	2. new
3. wishes	3. wrist
5. won't	4. sale
7. I'll	6. they've
8. wreath	9. fishes
10. blew	11. wreck
14. sail	12. dishes
15. wrench	13. I've

Test Practice for Lessons 16–20

T39	T40
A.	**B.**
Example: D) You'll	Example: B) coin
1. B) wren	1. A) sale
2. A) Wasn't	2. A) bushes
3. D) blew	3. B) sail
4. A) wrist	4. D) crushes
5. C) hear	5. A) washes
6. B) wrench	6. C) brushes
7. D) doesn't	7. D) fishes
8. C) Won't	8. B) flashes
9. B) wrong	9. C) knew

Review for Lessons 21–25

T41
A. 1. waxes   2. hair, hare

3. lives   4. heal, heel

B. 1. sixes, speeches, stitches, scratches, shelves

2. scratches

3. cities

C. branches, leaves, hare, babies or tail

T42

D. Across	Down
1. tail	2. axes
4. foxes	3. wolves
6. sow	5. ponies
8. matches	7. stitches
9. taxes	9. thieves
11. sew	10. hare

Test Practice for Lessons 21–25

T43	T44
A.	**B.**
Example: C) foxes	Example: A) stamp
1. C) taxes	1. D) ponies
2. A) catches	2. B) hair
3. C) waxes	3. A) thieves
4. B) stitches	4. C) knives
5. A) matches	5. D) guppies
6. D) babies	6. B) wolves
7. B) pennies	7. A) sew
8. A) mixes	8. D) heal
9. D) berries	9. B) tale

Review for Lessons 26–30

T45
A. 1. kisses   2. sheep   3. write, right

4. son, sun   5. no, know   6. men

7. bosses   8. geese

B. know, right, women, classes, someone/somebody, Somewhere

T46

C. Across	Down
2. children	1. mice
4. write	3. illnesses
6. sun	5. right
9. something	6. someday
10. hour	7. teeth
12. dresses	8. anyone
14. know	11. men
	13. son

Test Practice for Lessons 26–30

T47	T48
A.	**B.**
Example: A) losses	Example: B) cloud
1. D) glasses	1. A) someday
2. B) kisses	2. B) sun
3. C) oxen	3. C) somebody
4. D) women	4. C) anyway
5. B) teeth	5. D) anyplace
6. A) dresses	6. B) hour
7. A) know	7. B) somewhere
8. B) children	8. A) sometime
9. C) classes	9. C) our

Review for Lessons 1-5

A   **Write the spelling words that rhyme with the word pair.**

1. earn   learn   _____

2. perk   lurk   _____

3. verse   nurse   _____

4. serve   nerve   _____

5. tall   small   _____

6. gauze   laws   _____

B   **Fill in each blank with a spelling word.**

1. Write the word that is a month.   _____

2. Write the word that means a baby deer.   _____

3. What do babies do on hands and knees?   _____

C   **Use spelling words to complete the story.**

My sister doesn't like mornings. When I try to wake her,

she'll just _____ over and go back to sleep.

"Wake up, Sleeping Beauty!" I call out. "It's way past

_____."

"Mmph," she mumbles. Then she pulls the covers over her

head. Sometimes I send our dog in to wake her up.

Finally, she will _____ out of bed. She'll stumble

around and _____ out loud.

"It wouldn't _____ so hard to wake up," says my

sister, "if mornings began at noon."

her
fern
jerk
nerve
perch
verb
herd
perk
burst
turn
burn
nurse
church
curve
purse
curb
launch
gauze
vault
haul
fault
cause
haunt
August
red
read
not
knot
maid
made
be
bee
crawl
lawn
dawn
yawn
fawn
claw
flaw
straw

Name _____

Review for Lessons 1–5

D **Use spelling words to complete the puzzle.**

Across

1. an action word
3. where birds sit
5. mistake
6. a pouch for money
8. Fire does this.
9. a group of cattle
12. twist
13. grass in a yard

Down

2. a flying insect
4. opposite of "him"
5. a kind of plant
7. a color
8. to pop
10. I ___ a book on stars.
11. a tangle

her
fern
jerk
nerve
perch
verb
herd
perk
burst
turn
burn
nurse
church
curve
purse
curb
launch
gauze
vault
haul
fault
cause
haunt
August
red
read
not
knot
maid
made
be
bee
crawl
lawn
dawn
yawn
fawn
claw
flaw
straw

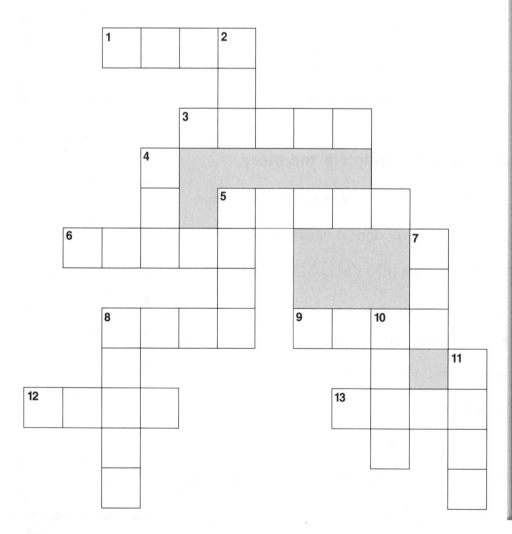

Name _____

Test Practice for Lessons 1–5

 A **Read each sentence. Find the correctly spelled word to complete it. Shade the letter next to the word.**

EXAMPLE

My _____ and I washed the car.

(A) dod   (B) dad   (C) ded   (D) dadd

---

1. A bird sits on a _____.

   (A) parch   (B) perch   (C) pirch   (D) perche

2. I turned the _____ too fast.

   (A) curyv   (B) carve   (C) corve   (D) curve

3. I put my money in the bank _____.

   (A) vaullt   (B) vualt   (C) vault   (D) valt

4. Did you water my _____?

   (A) furn   (B) fern   (C) farn   (D) furne

5. "I have some money in my _____," I said.

   (A) purse   (B) perse   (C) parse   (D) pirse

6. My mother used to _____ our coffee.

   (A) perke   (B) purk   (C) perk   (D) pirk

7. Be careful not to _____ yourself with a match.

   (A) burn   (B) burne   (C) birn   (D) bearn

8. Can I help you _____ away the trash?

   (A) hawl   (B) haul   (C) houl   (D) hawle

9. I saw a _____ of cattle on the road.

   (A) herde   (B) hearde   (C) hird   (D) herd

Name _____

Test Practice for Lessons 1–5

B **Find the correctly spelled word to complete each phrase. Shade the letter next to the correct word.**

> **EXAMPLE**
>
> swimming with my _____
>
> Ⓐ friend   Ⓑ frende   Ⓒ frind   Ⓓ freind

1. _____ that book

Ⓐ readd   Ⓑ red   Ⓒ raed   Ⓓ read

2. _____ the bed

Ⓐ made   Ⓑ maad   Ⓒ maed   Ⓓ mad

3. not my _____

Ⓐ foult   Ⓑ fault   Ⓒ faullt   Ⓓ folt

4. house made of _____

Ⓐ straw   Ⓑ strow   Ⓒ strawe   Ⓓ straew

5. tie a _____

Ⓐ knawt   Ⓑ knat   Ⓒ knot   Ⓓ knott

6. rise at _____

Ⓐ daln   Ⓑ dawwn   Ⓒ down   Ⓓ dawn

7. _____ like a baby

Ⓐ crawl   Ⓑ crowl   Ⓒ crall   Ⓓ craewl

8. _____ a problem

Ⓐ cawse   Ⓑ cuase   Ⓒ cause   Ⓓ cose

9. mow the _____

Ⓐ lwn   Ⓑ lan   Ⓒ lawn   Ⓓ lawyn

Name _____

Review for Lessons 6–10

A Write the spelling words that rhyme with the word pair.

1. cook   crook   _____

2. room   doom   _____

3. yield   shield   _____

4. great   date   _____

5. sail   fail   _____

B Which spelling word reads the same backward or forward?

_____

C Use spelling words to complete the story.

    I used to visit my grandmother on her farm. There was a lot of work to do, but it was fun.

    In the mornings, I would bring in _____ for the fireplace. Then I'd put some food in a _____ and feed the chickens. Grandmother would _____ me a big breakfast while I worked outside. After breakfast, I would go for a swim in the creek.

    Later I helped with the crops in the _____. The days were full of rich smells, hard work, and good food. I loved my trips to the farm.

foot
hook
wood
brook
stood
hood
crook
cook
food
noon
bloom
loose
booth
tooth
goose
proof
thief
chief
niece
piece
field
shield
brief
yield
road
rode
pail
pale
ate
eight
see
sea
breath
spread
thread
ready
feather
heavy
weather
leather

Name _____

Review for Lessons 6–10

 D **Use spelling words to complete the puzzle.**

Across

1. I lost my front ___.
3. It has five toes.
5. logs or lumber
8. comes after seven
9. street or highway
11. where crops are planted
12. a needle and ___
13. The traffic sign said ___.

Down

2. "Little Red Riding ___"
3. what we eat
4. a person who steals
6. The knight had a sword and ___.
7. air breathed in or out
10. The ___ is sunny and hot.

foot
hook
wood
brook
stood
hood
crook
cook
food
noon
bloom
loose
booth
tooth
goose
proof
thief
chief
niece
piece
field
shield
brief
yield
road
rode
pail
pale
ate
eight
see
sea
breath
spread
thread
ready
feather
heavy
weather
leather

Name _____

Test Practice for Lessons 6–10

 Read each sentence. Find the correctly spelled word to complete it. Shade the letter next to the word.

EXAMPLE

I will write a _____.

(A) lettr   (B) lettor   (C) leter   (D) letter

---

1. I tried not to step on her _____.

(A) foote   (B) foot   (C) foof   (D) fote

2. Did he lose a baby _____?

(A) tooth   (B) toth   (C) toeth   (D) tooyth

3. May I have a _____ of cake?

(A) peice   (B) peece   (C) peac   (D) piece

4. Did that _____ chase you?

(A) goase   (B) goose   (C) goos   (D) goese

5. I have _____ that my story is true.

(A) proof   (B) prof   (C) profe   (D) prooyf

6. "Has your _____ tooth come out yet?" she asked.

(A) lose   (B) loase   (C) loose   (D) loos

7. I like to eat lunch at 12 _____.

(A) noan   (B) noon   (C) noone   (D) nown

8. I called from the phone _____.

(A) booyth   (B) boothe   (C) boeth   (D) booth

9. I want to be the _____ of police.

(A) cheif   (B) chieph   (C) chief   (D) cheef

Name _____

Test Practice for Lessons 6–10

 B **Find the correctly spelled word to complete each phrase. Shade the letter next to the correct word.**

> **EXAMPLE**
>
> water under the _____
>
> Ⓐ brig   Ⓑ brige   Ⓒ bridge   Ⓓ briedge

1. _____ from bad weather

   Ⓐ sheild   Ⓑ shielt   Ⓒ shield   Ⓓ sheeld

2. _____ the fair rides

   Ⓐ roode   Ⓑ rode   Ⓒ roade   Ⓓ roed

3. went to bed at _____

   Ⓐ ieght   Ⓑ eihgt   Ⓒ eight   Ⓓ eaght

4. carrying a _____ bag

   Ⓐ hevy   Ⓑ heyvy   Ⓒ hevee   Ⓓ heavy

5. needle and _____

   Ⓐ thread   Ⓑ thraed   Ⓒ thred   Ⓓ threed

6. _____ to go home

   Ⓐ raddy   Ⓑ reidy   Ⓒ redy   Ⓓ ready

7. wearing a _____ belt

   Ⓐ laether   Ⓑ lether   Ⓒ leather   Ⓓ leether

8. a _____ of corn

   Ⓐ field   Ⓑ feald   Ⓒ feeld   Ⓓ fild

9. _____ a bad apple

   Ⓐ ate   Ⓑ aate   Ⓒ aet   Ⓓ aete

Name _____

Review for Lessons 11–15

A **Write the spelling words that rhyme with the word pair.**

1. cry   dry   _____

2. hour   sour   _____

3. ray   day   _____

4. block   sock   _____

5. do   shoe   _____

B **Fill in each blank with a spelling word.**

1. Which words end with *ght*?

    _____   _____   _____

2. Which words have the letter *w* in them?

    _____   _____

    _____   _____

C **Use spelling words to complete the story.**

Last night I went to bed _____. I was very tired.

The _____ wasn't even dark, but it only took a minute

or _____ for me to fall asleep.

I dreamed that I could _____. What a thrill it was!

I flew over rooftops and trees. I looked down and saw my

_____ waving at me. He wasn't even surprised to see

me flying.

When I woke up, I was disappointed. I didn't want my

flying dream _____ end.

Name _____

heard
learn
earn
pearl
earth
search
yearn
early
cry
fry
dry
shy
fly
sky
spy
pry
to
two
for
four
bear
bare
flour
flower
sleigh
freight
weigh
weight
neighbor
neigh
eighty
freighter
kneel
knock
knife
knit
knot
knob
knight
knack

Review for Lessons 11–15

 D **Use spelling words to complete the puzzle.**

Across

2. You ride in it in snow.

3. It opens a door.

5. to want something badly

7. a horse sound

8. babies may do this

9. where clouds are

11. dirt or ground

12. next-door ___

13. what you do at school

Down

1. A rose is one of these.

3. ___, fork, and spoon

4. comes after 79

6. a talent

10. to get down on your knees

11. opposite of "late"

heard
learn
earn
pearl
earth
search
yearn
early
cry
fry
dry
shy
fly
sky
spy
pry
to
two
for
four
bear
bare
flour
flower
sleigh
freight
weigh
weight
neighbor
neigh
eighty
freighter
kneel
knock
knife
knit
knot
knob
knight
knack

Name _____

Test Practice for Lessons 11–15

 A Read each sentence. Find the correctly spelled word to complete it. Shade the letter next to the word.

> **EXAMPLE**
>
> My mother likes to _____ sweaters.
>
> Ⓐ nitt   Ⓑ knitt   ● knit   Ⓓ kniet

1. I _____ the food here is good.

   Ⓐ haerd   Ⓑ herd   © heerd   Ⓓ heard

2. Did you _____ the potatoes?

   Ⓐ fri   Ⓑ frry   © fry   Ⓓ frie

3. Are there three or _____ little pigs?

   Ⓐ forr   Ⓑ four   © forye   Ⓓ for

4. How much money did we _____?

   Ⓐ earn   Ⓑ urne   © urn   Ⓓ earne

5. I am very _____ around people I don't know.

   Ⓐ shie   Ⓑ shye   © shy   Ⓓ shi

6. If I _____ long enough, I know I'll find it.

   Ⓐ searsh   Ⓑ serch   © seerch   Ⓓ search

7. Do you like to get up _____ or late?

   Ⓐ early   Ⓑ erly   © iarly   Ⓓ irly

8. I may _____ if I hear a sad story.

   Ⓐ cri   Ⓑ cry   © crie   Ⓓ criey

9. "The _____ is very blue today," he said.

   Ⓐ skiey   Ⓑ ski   © skie   Ⓓ sky

Name _____

Test Practice for Lessons 11–15

B **Find the correctly spelled word to complete each phrase. Shade the letter next to the correct word.**

> **EXAMPLE**
>
> a funny _____
>
> (A) joak   (B) joke   (C) joek   (D) jocke

1. _____ dollars more

   (A) atey   (B) eihgty   (C) eighty   (D) eaghty

2. turning the door _____

   (A) nob   (B) nawb   (C) knob   (D) knobb

3. the sharp _____

   (A) knife   (B) knief   (C) nife   (D) knif

4. _____ the fruit

   (A) waegh   (B) way   (C) wiegh   (D) weigh

5. a friendly _____

   (A) naybor   (B) neighbor   (C) neihgbor   (D) neeghbor

6. horses pulling the _____

   (A) slay   (B) sliegh   (C) sleigh   (D) slaey

7. _____ on the door

   (A) knock   (B) nawk   (C) knawk   (D) knoc

8. carrying _____ on a truck

   (A) frate   (B) frieght   (C) freight   (D) frayt

9. _____ for doing it right

   (A) nack   (B) knac   (C) knak   (D) knack

Name _____

Review for Lessons 16–20

A **Write the spelling words that rhyme with the word pair.**

1. bench   trench   _____

2. new   clue   _____

3. fishes   dishes   _____

4. dear   clear   _____

5. rushes   crushes   _____

6. mashes   lashes   _____

B **Use spelling words to complete the story.**

There are many ways to make a wish. People have made

_____ on stars and with wishbones. _____

thrown coins in fountains and wishing wells. On my birthday,

_____ make a wish when I blow out the candles on my

cake. Don't you wish that all of our wishes would come true?

C **Write the contractions for the underlined words.**

1. I will not be there.   _____

2. He will make a speech.   _____

3. That is not my book.   _____

4. I think you will win.   _____

5. She did not forget the cake.   _____

6. I hear they have found a cave.   _____

7. That does not make sense.   _____

wrench
wring
wrist
wrong
wreck
wrestle
wren
wreath
won't
aren't
isn't
doesn't
didn't
wasn't
hasn't
weren't
blew
blue
hear
here
sale
sail
knew
new
I'll
you'll
she'll
he'll
I've
you've
we've
they've
bushes
wishes
crushes
flashes
brushes
dishes
washes
fishes

Name _____

Review for Lessons 16–20

D Use spelling words to complete the puzzle.

Across

1. used to know
3. hopes or dreams
5. will not
7. I will
8. a door decoration
10. what wind did
14. to glide or float
15. a tool

Down

2. opposite of "old"
3. I wear a watch on my ___.
4. The house is for ___.
6. they have
9. He ___ for catfish.
11. a crash
12. plates and bowls
13. I have

wrench
wring
wrist
wrong
wreck
wrestle
wren
wreath
won't
aren't
isn't
doesn't
didn't
wasn't
hasn't
weren't
blew
blue
hear
here
sale
sail
knew
new
I'll
you'll
she'll
he'll
I've
you've
we've
they've
bushes
wishes
crushes
flashes
brushes
dishes
washes
fishes

Name _____

Test Practice for Lessons 16–20

A Read each sentence. Find the correctly spelled word to complete it. Shade the letter next to the word.

EXAMPLE

_____ want to go with us!

Ⓐ Youll   Ⓑ You'l   Ⓒ Youlle   ⬤ You'll

---

1. The _____ sings so nicely.

Ⓐ wrin   Ⓑ wren   Ⓒ ren   Ⓓ wrien

2. _____ that you on the phone?

Ⓐ Wasn't   Ⓑ Wassn't   Ⓒ Wosn't   Ⓓ Was'nt

3. The strong wind _____ the flagpole down.

Ⓐ blu   Ⓑ bluw   Ⓒ blue   Ⓓ blew

4. I put my new watch on my _____.

Ⓐ wrist   Ⓑ wriest   Ⓒ rist   Ⓓ wris

5. "I _____ you're coming to visit," she said.

Ⓐ hare   Ⓑ here   Ⓒ hear   Ⓓ her

6. I need a _____ to fix the car.

Ⓐ rench   Ⓑ wrench   Ⓒ wranch   Ⓓ wrinch

7. It _____ seem right to me.

Ⓐ does'nt   Ⓑ deosn't   Ⓒ dosn't   Ⓓ doesn't

8. _____ you come with us?

Ⓐ Want   Ⓑ Wan't   Ⓒ Won't   Ⓓ Wont

9. I may have the _____ answer.

Ⓐ wrng   Ⓑ wrong   Ⓒ wroang   Ⓓ rong

Name _____

Test Practice for Lessons 16–20

B Find the correctly spelled word to complete each phrase. Shade the letter next to the correct word.

EXAMPLE

toss of the _____

(A) coine   (B) coin   (C) coyn   (D) cone

---

1. clothes on _____

(A) sale   (B) sael   (C) salle   (D) sayl

2. trim the _____

(A) bushes   (B) bueshes   (C) booshes   (D) bushez

3. _____ the seven seas

(A) saiyl   (B) sail   (C) sayle   (D) saill

4. _____ the cans

(A) cruwshes   (B) crushez   (C) crushs   (D) crushes

5. _____ the dishes

(A) washes   (B) washez   (C) waeshes   (D) washs

6. _____ her hair often

(A) brushez   (B) brueshes   (C) brushes   (D) breshes

7. _____ at that pond

(A) feshes   (B) fishez   (C) fieshes   (D) fishes

8. camera _____

(A) flashez   (B) flashes   (C) flashs   (D) flaeshes

9. _____ he was coming

(A) knwe   (B) knaw   (C) knew   (D) knue

Name _____

Review for Lessons 21–25

A Write the spelling words that rhyme with the word pair.

1. axes   taxes   _____

2. bear   dare   _____

3. wives   knives   _____

4. meal   deal   _____

B Fill in each blank with a spelling word.

1. Which words begin and end with *s*?

   _____   _____   _____

   _____   _____

2. Which word has the most letters? _____

3. Which word has two *i*'s? _____

C Use spelling words to complete the story.

Our house is at the edge of town. We live near a big

forest. Each day I go for a walk in the forest.

I like to climb the trees and sit on the _____.

I look through the green _____ at the ground below.

One day I saw a _____ with long brown ears.

I watched it hop under a bush. I could see the hare's

_____ sticking out of the bush. It's fun to see all

the creatures in the forest.

---

boxes
foxes
fixes
waxes
taxes
axes
mixes
sixes
branches
speeches
stitches
scratches
churches
catches
crutches
matches
pennies
babies
cherries
berries
ponies
puppies
cities
guppies
hare
hair
tail
tale
sew
sow
heal
heel
leaves
wolves
knives
calves
shelves
thieves
loaves
lives

Name _____

Review for Lessons 21–25

D Use spelling words to complete the puzzle.

Across

1. a dog wags it
4. bushy-tailed animals
6. to plant seeds
8. They can start fires.
9. money paid to the government
11. Can you ___ my torn shirt?

Down

2. chopping tools
3. wild animals of the dog family
5. small horses
7. sews
9. robbers
10. rabbit

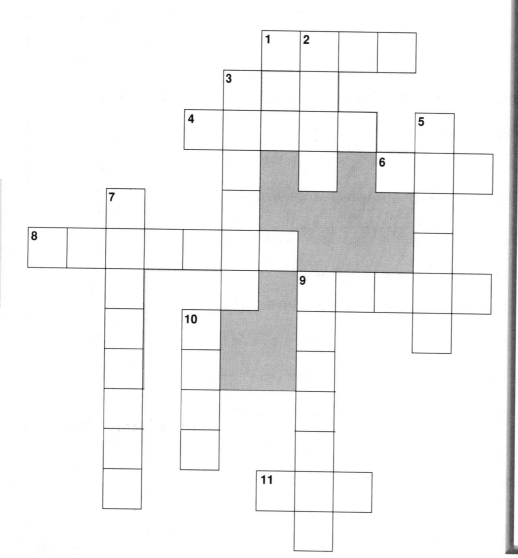

boxes
foxes
fixes
waxes
taxes
axes
mixes
sixes
branches
speeches
stitches
scratches
churches
catches
crutches
matches
pennies
babies
cherries
berries
ponies
puppies
cities
guppies
hare
hair
tail
tale
sew
sow
heal
heel
leaves
wolves
knives
calves
shelves
thieves
loaves
lives

Name _____

Test Practice for Lessons 21–25

 A **Read each sentence. Find the correctly spelled word to complete it. Shade the letter next to the word.**

> **EXAMPLE**
>
> I saw three _____ in my backyard.
>
> Ⓐ foexes   Ⓑ fockses   ⬤ foxes   Ⓓ foxsez

1. You will have to pay _____ on those boxes.

   Ⓐ taxzez   Ⓑ tixes   © taxes   Ⓓ tacxes

2. She _____ those fly balls well.

   Ⓐ catches   Ⓑ cachez   © catshes   Ⓓ caches

3. The floor shines when he _____ it.

   Ⓐ waxez   Ⓑ waches   © waxes   Ⓓ waksez

4. I had to have ten _____ in my leg.

   Ⓐ stitshes   Ⓑ stitches   © stiches   Ⓓ steches

5. We need dry _____ for the fire.

   Ⓐ matches   Ⓑ matshes   © mathes   Ⓓ maches

6. How old are the little _____?

   Ⓐ babeies   Ⓑ babeez   © baybies   Ⓓ babies

7. Five _____ make a nickel.

   Ⓐ pineze   Ⓑ pennies   © pannies   Ⓓ pinnies

8. He always _____ sugar with his iced tea.

   Ⓐ mixes   Ⓑ micses   © mixses   Ⓓ miksez

9. Please help me pick all these _____ on the vine.

   Ⓐ beries   Ⓑ bearries   © barries   Ⓓ berries

Name _____

Test Practice for Lessons 21–25

B Find the correctly spelled word to complete each phrase. Shade the letter next to the correct word.

EXAMPLE

a _____ collection

(A) stamp   (B) stanp   (C) stap   (D) stampp

---

1. _____ in the barn

   (A) poenies   (B) ponnies   (C) poneze   (D) ponies

2. the _____ on your head

   (A) hare   (B) hair   (C) heir   (D) haer

3. _____ going to jail

   (A) thieves   (B) theives   (C) thiefz   (D) thefes

4. _____ used for cutting

   (A) knieves   (B) nives   (C) knives   (D) knivez

5. _____ in the fish tank

   (A) guppeze   (B) gappies   (C) guppiez   (D) guppies

6. feed it to the_____

   (A) wolvz   (B) wolves   (C) walves   (D) woolves

7. _____ buttons on coats

   (A) sew   (B) sow   (C) so   (D) sowe

8. _____ the sore foot

   (A) hill   (B) heele   (C) heel   (D) heal

9. telling a tall _____

   (A) tell   (B) tale   (C) tail   (D) tayl

Name _____

Review for Lessons 26–30

A **Write the spelling words that rhyme with the word pair.**

1. hisses   misses   _____

2. beep   keep   _____

3. might   tight   _____

4. bun   run   _____

5. so   grow   _____

6. den   ten   _____

7. losses   tosses   _____

8. peace   cease   _____

B **Use spelling words to complete the story.**

We all _____ that school can be hard. But it

helps to have a special teacher who sees you through the

hard times.

Not every teacher is _____ for each student. It

doesn't matter if teachers are men or _____. What

really matters is that they care about the students in their

_____.

I remember a teacher that I called "Mrs. Y." She was

_____ who made a big difference in my life. She

taught me how to open my eyes to the world. I've had many

good teachers, but Mrs. Y is the one I'll never forget.

_____ out there is Mrs Y. If I saw her today,

I would thank her for being so wonderful!

Name _____

dresses
bosses
illnesses
classes
glasses
guesses
kisses
losses
men
women
children
teeth
mice
oxen
sheep
geese
know
no
write
right
hour
our
son
sun
anyone
anything
anybody
anyplace
anyhow
anywhere
anyway
anytime
someone
something
somebody
someplace
somehow
somewhere
sometime
someday

Review for Lessons 26–30

 Use spelling words to complete the puzzle.

Across

2. boys and girls
4. You do this with paper and pen.
6. the star nearest Earth
9. I have ___ to tell you.
10. sixty minutes
12. more than one dress
14. understand

Down

1. Cats like to catch ___.
3. sicknesses
5. opposite of "wrong"
6. We'll meet again ___.
7. what dentists take care of
8. any person
11. what boys grow up to be
13. daughter and ___

dresses
bosses
illnesses
classes
glasses
guesses
kisses
losses
men
women
children
teeth
mice
oxen
sheep
geese
know
no
write
right
hour
our
son
sun
anyone
anything
anybody
anyplace
anyhow
anywhere
anyway
anytime
someone
something
somebody
someplace
somehow
somewhere
sometime
someday

Name _____

Test Practice for Lessons 26–30

 A Read each sentence. Find the correctly spelled word to complete it. Shade the letter next to the word.

EXAMPLE

The team was not happy about their _____.

🅐 losses   Ⓑ loesses   Ⓒ lossez   Ⓓ loses

1. Don't drink out of dirty _____.

Ⓐ glaesses   Ⓑ glassez   Ⓒ glosses   Ⓓ glasses

2. She _____ her babies all the time.

Ⓐ kesses   Ⓑ kisses   Ⓒ kasses   Ⓓ kissez

3. Some people use _____ to plow fields.

Ⓐ auxen   Ⓑ oxenn   Ⓒ oxen   Ⓓ oxin

4. The _____ joined a new tennis club.

Ⓐ wemen   Ⓑ woeman   Ⓒ weemen   Ⓓ women

5. "Did you have any _____ pulled?" my friend asked.

Ⓐ teath   Ⓑ teeth   Ⓒ teith   Ⓓ teethe

6. She designs _____ for a living.

Ⓐ dresses   Ⓑ dressez   Ⓒ dreses   Ⓓ dreases

7. I _____ what will help us win.

Ⓐ know   Ⓑ now   Ⓒ knoe   Ⓓ noe

8. The _____ all went out to play.

Ⓐ cheldren   Ⓑ children   Ⓒ chilldren   Ⓓ childrin

9. How many _____ are you taking now?

Ⓐ classez   Ⓑ closses   Ⓒ classes   Ⓓ clases

Name _____

Test Practice for Lessons 26–30

B Find the correctly spelled word to complete each phrase. Shade the letter next to the correct word.

EXAMPLE

a _____ in the sky

Ⓐ clowd   🅑 cloud   Ⓒ clowde   Ⓓ cload

---

1. _____ we'll go

Ⓐ someday   Ⓑ sumday   Ⓒ somedaye   Ⓓ somday

2. the warm _____

Ⓐ suun   Ⓑ sun   Ⓒ suen   Ⓓ suun

3. help _____ out

Ⓐ somebady   Ⓑ sombody   Ⓒ somebody   Ⓓ sumbody

4. can't go home _____

Ⓐ enyway   Ⓑ anywag   Ⓒ anyway   Ⓓ inyway

5. _____ to go

Ⓐ anyplase   Ⓑ enyplace   Ⓒ inyplace   Ⓓ anyplace

6. clock set to the _____

Ⓐ our   Ⓑ hour   Ⓒ huor   Ⓓ howr

7. _____ over the rainbow

Ⓐ somewear   Ⓑ somewhere   Ⓒ samewhere   Ⓓ somwhere

8. _____ in the afternoon

Ⓐ sometime   Ⓑ sametime   Ⓒ somtime   Ⓓ sumtime

9. _____ own town

Ⓐ awr   Ⓑ owr   Ⓒ our   Ⓓ ourr

Name _____

STECK-VAUGHN

Target
SPELLING 780

Margaret Scarborough
Mary F. Brigham
Teresa A. Miller

STECK-VAUGHN
ELEMENTARY · SECONDARY · ADULT · LIBRARY

A Harcourt Company

www.steck-vaughn.com

Table of Contents

Acknowledgments

Editorial Director: Stephanie Muller
Editor: Kathleen Gower Wiseman
Associate Director of Design: Cynthia Ellis
Design Managers: Sheryl Cota, Katie Nott
Illustrators: Peg Dougherty, Jimmy Longacre, Cindy Aarvig, David Griffin, Lynn McClain
Cover Design: Bassett & Brush Design, Todd Disrud and Stephanie Schreiber

ISBN 0-7398-2459-7

Copyright © 2001 Steck-Vaughn Company

5 6 7 8 9   054   07 06 05 04 03

Word Study Plan

1 **LOOK** at the word. _____

2 **SAY** the word. _____

3 **THINK** about each letter. _____

4 **SPELL** the word aloud. _____

5 **WRITE** the word. _____

6 **CHECK** the spelling. _____

7 **REPEAT** the steps
if you need more practice. _____

Name _____

Spelling Strategies

shown
shipped
shopped

pair, fair, hair

Think about the beginning sound of the word that you want to spell. Then think about a word you know that begins with the same sound.

Look for word families. The first letters of the words in a word family are different. The other letters are the same. Words in a word family rhyme.

Think about the shape of each letter in the word.

p i c k l e

If you are not sure how to spell a word, take a guess. Then look up the word in the dictionary.

Think about how a word is spelled and then write it. Try different spellings. Look at each spelling to see if it looks right.

peeceful
peaceful ✓
peacful

sub•ur•ban

Lesson 1   Words with *er*

her	jerk	perch	herd
fern	nerve	verb	perk

A   **Fill in each blank with a spelling word.**

1. She felt sick, so I took _____her_____ some soup.

2. A _____fern_____ is a nice plant to grow.

3. It takes _____nerve_____ to be a firefighter.

4. The bird is resting on its _____perch_____.

5. The carnival ride made me _____jerk_____ from side to side.

6. An action word is called a _____verb_____.

7. The coffee is about to _____perk_____.

8. A _____herd_____ of wild horses ran through the field.

B   **Circle the word that is the same as the top one.**

her	fern	jerk	nerve	perch	verb	herd	perk
him	fenn	(jerk)	rerve	porch	werb	berd	(perk)
hen	fenr	jark	nirve	(perch)	verd	(herd)	pork
yer	(fern)	jarh	narve	qerch	(verb)	herb	park
(her)	farn	yerk	(nerve)	pench	vorb	harb	qerk

C   **Write a spelling word under each picture.**

1. _____fern_____   2. _____perch_____   3. _____perk_____

Name _____

Words with *er*

her	jerk	perch	herd
fern	nerve	verb	perk

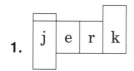

A **Fill in the boxes with the correct spelling words.**
Note: In this type of exercise, the configuration of some words may be the same.

1. | j | e | r | k |

2. | h | e | r | d |

3. | f | e | r | n |

4. | h | e | r |

5. | p | e | r | c | h |

6. | n | e | r | v | e |

B **Write the spelling word that rhymes with the word pair.**

1. turn   learn   _____fern_____

2. curve   swerve   _____nerve_____

3. lurk   perk   _____jerk_____

4. bird   word   _____herd_____

C **Write each spelling word beside its clue.**

fern   1. a plant that likes wet places

nerve   2. courage

her   3. goes with "she"

perch   4. a pole or rod for a bird to rest on

herd   5. many animals in a group

perk   6. to become lively

jerk   7. a quick, sharp pull or twist

verb   8. a word that shows action

DAY 3

Words with *er*

her	jerk	perch	herd
fern	nerve	verb	perk

A Find the missing letters. Then write the word.

1. v __e__ __r__ b   __verb__

2. n __e__ r v __e__   __nerve__

B Write the spelling words in alphabetical (ABC) order.

1. __fern__   2. __her__   3. __herd__   4. __jerk__

5. __nerve__   6. __perch__   7. __perk__   8. __verb__

C Use the correct spelling words to complete the story.

The cowboys who went on trail drives years ago are the real heroes of the West. They would move a __herd__ of cattle from the South to the North. Most cattle trails ended in Kansas. There the beef from the herd was sent east by train.

Trail drives were full of danger and lasted for months. The weather wasn't always good, and thieves would try to steal herds. At night, one cowboy would __perch__ on his horse to watch for thieves while the other cowboys slept.

It took __nerve__ to be a cowboy on trail drives.

D Complete each sentence.

Note: Annotated answers are provided only for exercises which require students to choose among answers.

1. It's her turn to _____.

2. The fern I bought is _____.

Name _____

DAY
4

Words with *er*

her	jerk	perch	herd
fern	nerve	verb	perk

A **Fill in each blank with a spelling word.**

1. Write the words that begin with *per.*

   ___perch___   ___perk___

2. Write the words that begin with *h.*

   ___her___   ___herd___

3. Write the word that ends with a vowel. ___nerve___

B **Use the correct spelling words to answer these riddles.**

1. This is a sharp pull, push, or bounce.

   What is it? ___jerk___

2. This is the courage you need to take a test. It also names a type of fiber in your body.

   What is it? ___nerve___

3. Birds like to rest on this. It can also be a kind of fish.

   What is it? ___perch___

C **Use each spelling word in a sentence.**

herd _____

nerve _____

perk _____

fern _____

verb _____

Lesson 2 Words with *ur*

DAY 1

turn	purse	burst	church
burn	nurse	curve	curb

A **Fill in each blank with a spelling word.**

1. The wedding was held in the ____church____.

2. The ____nurse____ in the hospital was very nice to me.

3. It's my ____turn____ to do the dishes.

4. The balloon ____burst____ from too much air.

5. When a line bends, it's called a ____curve____.

6. Don't ____burn____ your hand on the hot stove!

7. We stood on the ____curb____ before crossing the street.

8. Do you have a pen in your ____purse____?

B **Circle the letters that are the same in all the spelling words.**

b(ur)st   t(ur)n   b(ur)n   n(ur)se   ch(ur)ch   c(ur)ve   p(ur)se   c(ur)b

C **Write the spelling words that rhyme with the word pair.**

1. first   thirst   ____burst_____

2. fern   churn   ____turn, burn____

3. verse   worse   ____nurse, purse____

4. search   perch   ____church____

5. herb   verb   ____curb____

D **Complete the sentence.**

The balloon <u>burst</u> _____.

Name _____

Lesson 2

DAY 2

Words with *ur*

turn	purse	burst	church
burn	nurse	curve	curb

A Circle the word that is the same as the top one.

burst	turn	burn	nurse	church	curve	purse	curb
(burst)	tunn	durn	nnrse	(church)	carve	qurse	carb
bursh	tunr	(burn)	(nurse)	cburch	cnrve	porse	curd
burts	furn	barn	narse	charch	(curve)	parse	(curb)
burns	(turn)	bunn	nunse	chorch	corve	(purse)	cunb

B Answer the questions with spelling words.

1. Which word means "to explode or break open"? _____burst_____

2. Which word means "a small bag or pouch"? _____purse_____

3. Which word means "the edge of a street"? _____curb_____

4. Which word means "to be on fire"? _____burn_____

5. Which word means "a bending line"? _____curve_____

C Fill in the boxes with the correct spelling words.

1. | n | u | r | s | e |

2. | c | u | r | b |

3. | c | u | r | v | e |

4. | b | u | r | s | t |

5. | t | u | r | n | burn

6. | c | h | u | r | c | h |

D Find the missing letters. Then write the word.

1. c h _u_ _r_ _c_ _h_   _____church_____

2. p _u_ _r_ s e   _____purse_____

8

DAY 3

Words with *ur*

turn	purse	burst	church
burn	nurse	curve	curb

A Use spelling words in two sentences.

1. _____

2. _____

B Use the correct spelling words to complete the story.

I will never forget the first time I rode with my brother in his car. He was the best driver I had ever seen.

He had just bought a new car, and he wanted to take me for a drive. My brother never forgot to signal before he was about to ___turn___ a corner. He stopped at the stop light near the old, stone ___church___. If a street began to ___curve___, he gently stepped on the brakes. And when he pulled up next to the ___curb___, he didn't even bump it! Someday I hope that I will drive as well as my brother.

C Write the spelling words in alphabetical order.

1. ___burn___ 2. ___burst___ 3. ___church___ 4. ___curb___

5. ___curve___ 6. ___nurse___ 7. ___purse___ 8. ___turn___

D Write the spelling words that have five letters.

___burst___ ___purse___

___nurse___ ___curve___

Name _____

Lesson 2

Words with *ur*

turn	purse	burst	church
burn	nurse	curve	curb

A One word is wrong in each sentence. Circle the wrong word. Then fill in the blank with a spelling word that makes sense.

1. The (clown) gave me a shot in my arm.   _nurse_

2. The balloon (cried) from having too much air.   _burst_

3. You light a candle so that it will (walk.)   _burn_

4. She keeps her wallet in her (garden.)   _purse_

B Write a spelling word under each picture.

1. _purse_   2. _church_   3. _curve_

C Answer the questions with spelling words.

1. Which word begins and ends with the same sound?

   church

2. Which words end with silent *e*?

   nurse   _purse_   _curve_

3. Which words have the letter *b* in them?

   burst   _burn_   _curb_

4. Which words end in *urn*?

   burn   _turn_

Words with *au*

launch	vault	fault	haunt
gauze	haul	cause	August

A **Fill in each blank with a spelling word.**

1. Please put my money in the bank's ____vault____.

2. We need to ____haul____ away all of the empty boxes.

3. It's my ____fault____ that we were late.

4. The space center will ____launch____ a new rocket.

5. What was the ____cause____ of the fire?

6. You wrap a burn in a ____gauze____ bandage.

7. The story says that a noisy ghost may ____haunt____ the old house.

8. ____August____ is the eighth month of the year.

B **Find the missing letters. Then write the word.**

1. v _a_ _u_ l t   ____vault____

2. _A_ _u_ g u s t   ____August____

C **Circle the letters that are the same in all the spelling words.**

l(au)nch   g(au)ze   v(au)lt   h(au)l   f(au)lt   c(au)se   h(au)nt   (Au)gust

D **Write the spelling words in alphabetical order.**

1. ____August____ 2. ____cause____ 3. ____fault____ 4. ____gauze____

5. ____haul____ 6. ____haunt____ 7. ____launch____ 8. ____vault____

Name _____

Lesson 3

Words with *au*

launch	vault	fault	haunt
gauze	haul	cause	August

A Use the correct spelling words to complete the story.

Have you ever seen the ___launch___ of a rocket? We saw one

launched last ___August___. It was the best part of my summer. If you

think a rocket looks big on TV, you should see the real thing!

It takes a few days just to ___haul___ a rocket to the launch pad.

When it takes off, the power and noise ___cause___ the ground to rumble

and shake.

B Write each spelling word beside its clue.

___launch___   **1.** to send off or set in motion

___haunt___   **2.** to disturb

___vault___   **3.** a room in a bank

___gauze___   **4.** a piece of cloth used in first aid

___August___   **5.** the name of a month

___fault___   **6.** blame

___haul___   **7.** to carry

___cause___   **8.** something that brings about a result

C Write the spelling words that name things you <u>cannot</u> touch.

1. ___launch___   2. ___haul___   3. ___cause___

4. ___August___   5. ___fault___   6. ___haunt___

Words with *au*

launch	vault	fault	haunt
gauze	haul	cause	August

A Circle the word that is the same as the top one.

launch	gauze	vault	haul	fault	cause	haunt	August
luanch	gouze	(vault)	baul	tault	couse	(haunt)	Aagust
lauuch	(gauze)	vaulf	hual	faulf	(cause)	baunt	Augusf
(launch)	pauze	voult	(haul)	fualt	cauze	haunf	(August)
leunch	guaze	wault	houl	(fault)	cuase	hount	Aujust

B Write the spelling words that rhyme with the word pair.

1. laws   saws   _cause, gauze_

2. fall   call   _haul_

3. malt   salt   _vault, fault_

4. want   jaunt   _haunt_

C Use each spelling word in a sentence.

launch _____

gauze _____

vault _____

haul _____

fault _____

cause _____

haunt _____

August _____

Name _____

Words with *au*

launch	vault	fault	haunt
gauze	haul	cause	August

A Find each hidden word from the list.

launch	vault	fault	haunt
gauze	haul	cause	August
law	draw	how	plow

```
u  r  l  a  u  n  c  h  m  y  l  b  e  s  t  h  f
r  i  e  u  n  d  w  h  y  d  a  o  n  d  r  a  w
t  w  v  g  a  u  z  e  h  o  w  e  g  o  o  u  t
t  f  a  u  l  t  o  s  a  w  i  m  o  r  g  l  o
f  o  u  s  r  a  c  a  u  r  r  i  d  e  i  n  y
o  u  l  t  r  n  e  w  n  l  i  t  p  l  o  w  t
l  e  t  s  p  o  r  t  t  s  c  a  u  s  e  c  o
u  l  d  h  a  v  e  a  l  o  t  o  f  f  u  n  i
```

B Answer the questions with spelling words.

1. Which word begins with a capital letter? ___August___

2. Which words end with a silent *e*?

   ___gauze___   ___cause___

3. Which words begin with the same first letter?

   ___haul___   ___haunt___

4. Which words end with *ult*?

   ___vault___   ___fault___

5. Which word ends with *ch*?

   ___launch___

Lesson 4   Homonyms

red	not	maid	be
read	knot	made	bee

A **Fill in each blank with a spelling word.**

1. I _____read_____ about you in the newspaper.

2. Can you tie a _____knot_____ in the rope?

3. The _____maid_____ will clean up the hotel room.

4. She _____made_____ me a great birthday cake.

5. I am _____not_____ going to the party on Friday.

6. When the light turns _____red_____, you have to stop.

7. Will you _____be_____ my valentine?

8. A _____bee_____ stung me on my foot!

B **Find the missing letters. Then write the word.**

1. m _a_ _i_ d   _____maid_____

2. m _a_ _d_ e   _____made_____

3. r _e_ _a_ d   _____read_____

4. _k_ _n_ _o_ t   _____knot_____

C **Write a spelling word under each picture.**

1. _____knot_____   2. _____read_____   3. _____bee_____

Name _____

Homonyms

red	not	maid	be
read	knot	made	bee

A Fill in the boxes with the correct spelling words.

1. r e d

2. m a d e

3. n o t

4. b e

5. k n o t

6. m a i d

7. r e a d

8. b e e

B Write each spelling word beside its clue.

read _____ **1.** what you do with a book

made _____ **2.** caused something to be or to happen

knot _____ **3.** something tied together, or a tangle

red _____ **4.** traffic light color that means "stop"

bee _____ **5.** an insect that makes honey

maid _____ **6.** the homonym for "made"

C Use the correct spelling words to complete the story.

My aunt was hanging out clothes on the line, when a ____bee____ stung her.

"Ouch!" she cried. She ran inside, holding her arm. The bee's sting ____made____ a big purple and ____red____ knot.

She found a first-aid book and ____read____ that you should try to ____be____ calm, remove the stinger, and put medicine on the knot. After my aunt did that, she felt much better.

Homonyms

red	not	maid	be
read	knot	made	bee

A **Fill in each blank with a spelling word.**

1. Write the words that end with *d*.

   <u>   red   </u>   <u>   read   </u>   <u>   maid   </u>

2. Write the word that ends with two *e*'s. <u>   bee   </u>

3. Write the words that have the letter *o*.

   <u>   not   </u>   <u>   knot   </u>

B **Write the spelling words that rhyme with the word pair.**

1. paid   raid   <u>made, maid</u>

2. lot   cot   <u>not, knot</u>

3. see   me   <u>be, bee</u>

4. fed   bed   <u>red, read</u>

C **Use each spelling word in a sentence.**

red   _____

read   _____

not   _____

knot   _____

maid   _____

made   _____

be   _____

bee   _____

Name _____

Lesson 4 Homonyms

DAY 4

red	not	maid	be
read	knot	made	bee

A Find each hidden word from the list.

red	not	maid	be
read	knot	made	bee
oil	spoil	coin	join

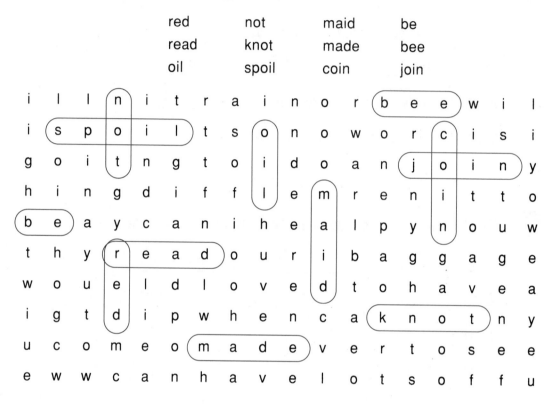

B Write the spelling words in alphabetical order.

1. _____be_____ 2. _____bee_____ 3. _____knot_____ 4. _____made_____

5. _____maid_____ 6. _____not_____ 7. _____read_____ 8. _____red_____

C Fill in each blank with a spelling word.

1. Write the word that names a color. _____red_____

2. Write the word that starts with a silent letter. _____knot_____

3. Write the word that names a flying insect. _____bee_____

4. Write the word that has only two letters. _____be_____

18

Lesson 5

Words with *aw*

crawl	dawn	fawn	flaw
lawn	yawn	claw	straw

A **Fill in each blank with a spelling word.**

1. Yesterday we saw a mother deer and her ___fawn___ in the woods behind our house.

2. People ___yawn___ when they are tired.

3. Will you help me mow the ___lawn___?

4. My brother wakes up at the crack of ___dawn___.

5. I had to ___crawl___ under the table to find my glasses.

6. A mistake in something is called a ___flaw___.

7. My new hat is made out of ___straw___.

8. The cat's ___claw___ is very sharp.

B **Write the spelling words that end in *aw*.**

___claw___ ___flaw___ ___straw___

C **Fill in the boxes with the correct spelling words.**

1. | c | l | a | w |

2. | f | l | a | w |

3. | y | a | w | n |

4. | l | a | w | n |

5. | f | a | w | n |

6. | s | t | r | a | w |

7. | c | r | a | w | l |

8. | d | a | w | n |

Name _____

Lesson 5 — Words with *aw*

DAY 2

crawl	dawn	fawn	flaw
lawn	yawn	claw	straw

A Circle the word that is the same as the top one.

crawl	lawn	dawn	yawn	fawn	claw	flaw	straw
craml	lown	bawn	(yawn)	famn	clow	flow	strow
(crawl)	lamn	(dawn)	gawn	bawn	(claw)	flam	sfraw
cnawl	(lawn)	down	yown	(fawn)	clam	falw	(straw)
crowl	lewn	bamn	yawr	fown	clau	(flaw)	srtaw

B Write the spelling words in alphabetical order.

1. claw 2. crawl 3. dawn 4. fawn

5. flaw 6. lawn 7. straw 8. yawn

C Write each spelling word beside its clue.

straw   **1.** a thin tube to drink through

crawl   **2.** what babies do before they walk

fawn   **3.** a baby deer

yawn   **4.** what people do when they are tired

dawn   **5.** the first light of the morning

flaw   **6.** a mistake

claw   **7.** a sharp nail on a cat's paw

lawn   **8.** the part of a yard that is usually mowed

20

Lesson 5

Words with *aw*

crawl	dawn	fawn	flaw
lawn	yawn	claw	straw

A Find the missing letters. Then write the word.

1. c r <u>a</u> <u>w</u> <u>l</u>   <u>crawl</u>

2. s t <u>r</u> <u>a</u> <u>w</u>   <u>straw</u>

B Write a spelling word under each picture.

1. <u>yawn</u>   2. <u>crawl</u>   3. <u>claw</u>

C Write the spelling words that rhyme with the word pair.

1. lawn   yawn   <u>dawn, fawn</u>

2. flaw   straw   <u>claw</u>

3. drawl   brawl   <u>crawl</u>

D Circle the letters that are the same in all the spelling words.

cr(aw)l   l(aw)n   d(aw)n   y(aw)n   f(aw)n   cl(aw)   fl(aw)   str(aw)

E Complete each sentence.

1. We had to <u>crawl</u> _____.

2. I woke up at <u>dawn</u> and _____.

3. He found a <u>flaw</u> in _____.

Name _____

DAY 4

Words with *aw*

crawl	dawn	fawn	flaw
lawn	yawn	claw	straw

A **Use the correct spelling words to complete the story.**

I awoke at _____dawn_____ to a chorus of terrible sounds. I heard

hissing and spitting and growling. Two cats were having a fight outside.

I had never heard such a racket before! I jumped out of bed and ran

downstairs.

I grabbed a broom made of _____straw_____ and went outside to stop the

fight. The cats were on my front _____lawn_____. They turned to look at me.

Then one cat tried to _____claw_____ the other. I shouted, "Stop!" Both cats

sped out of my yard.

I saw one _____crawl_____ under a house. The other cat ran down the street.

What a way to start the day!

B **Use each spelling word in a sentence.**

crawl _____

lawn _____

dawn _____

yawn _____

fawn _____

claw _____

flaw _____

straw _____

her	perch	burst	church	launch
fern	verb	turn	curve	gauze
jerk	herd	burn	purse	vault
nerve	perk	nurse	curb	haul

A **Write a spelling word under each picture.**

1. _____church_____   2. _____purse_____   3. _____fern_____

B **Fill in each blank with a spelling word.**

1. The bird sat on its _____perch_____.

2. Buffaloes run in a _____herd_____.

3. The balloon had too much air and _____burst_____.

4. The car slowed down around the _____curve_____.

5. _____Her_____ new hat is very pretty.

6. When I get sick, I call my friend who is a _____nurse_____.

7. Did you _____haul_____ away the trash?

8. They will _____launch_____ the rocket tomorrow.

9. Please _____turn_____ left at the light.

10. The bank puts the money in the _____vault_____.

11. Can you find the noun and the _____verb_____ in that sentence?

12. I will put a piece of _____gauze_____ over the scrape.

Name _____

fault	red	maid	crawl	fawn
cause	read	made	lawn	claw
haunt	not	be	dawn	flaw
August	knot	bee	yawn	straw

C **Write the spelling words that rhyme with the word pair.**

1. law   flaw   <u>claw, straw</u>

2. free   tree   <u>bee, be</u>

3. hot   rot   <u>not, knot</u>

4. saws   pause   <u>cause</u>

5. lawn   dawn   <u>yawn, fawn</u>

D **Use the correct spelling words to complete the story.**

Last year I went to visit my friend. It was in the month of <u>August</u>.

One night my friend told me a story about a haunted house. She had <u>read</u>

the story in a book.

The story said that there was a strange house on a hill. The neighbors that

lived near the house always heard loud noises coming from it. When they went to

see what was making the loud noises, no one would be there. They also saw

lights flashing on and off in the house. Sometimes they would see a blue or

<u>red</u> light that was shining on the porch. This always <u>made</u>

them feel funny. The noises would last all night long and then stop at

<u>dawn</u>. They never did find out what it was that made the loud noises. If

I had lived near that house, I don't think I would even want to know!

Words with *oo*

foot	wood	stood	crook
hook	brook	hood	cook

A **Fill in each blank with a spelling word.**

1. The water in the little _____brook_____ was cold.

2. Let's bring some _____wood_____ in for the fire.

3. You have to put bait on the _____hook_____ to catch a fish.

4. I _____stood_____ up to see my friend score the goal.

5. The _____hood_____ of a car covers the engine.

6. He fell down and broke his _____foot_____.

7. The _____cook_____ did not burn the food.

8. The curved part of an umbrella handle is called a _____crook_____.

B **Find the missing letters. Then write the word.**

1. s t _o_ _o_ d _____stood_____

2. c _r_ _o_ _o_ k _____crook_____

C **Circle the letters that are the same in all the spelling words.**

f(oo)t   h(oo)k   w(oo)d   br(oo)k   st(oo)d   h(oo)d   cr(oo)k   c(oo)k

D **One word is wrong in each sentence. Circle the wrong word. Then fill in the blank with a spelling word that makes sense.**

1. I caught the fish on a (toothpick.) _____hook_____

2. We need (water) to make the fire burn. _____wood_____

3. You should thank the (plate) for the food we ate. _____cook_____

4. We all (flew) up when our team scored. _____stood_____

Name _____

Words with *oo*

foot	wood	stood	crook
hook	brook	hood	cook

A **Circle the word that is the same as the top one.**

foot	hook	wood	brook	stood	hood	crook	cook
foof	book	mood	bnook	sfood	(hood)	cnook	dook
feet	(hook)	woob	breek	(stood)	heed	(crook)	beek
toof	heek	(wood)	drook	stoob	hoob	creek	booh
(foot)	hooh	weed	(brook)	steed	bood	croak	(cook)

B **Write the spelling words that rhyme with the word pair.**

1. hook   crook   brook, cook

2. soot   put   foot

3. hood   stood   wood

4. brook   cook   hook, crook

5. wood   hood   stood

C **Write the spelling words that name things you can touch.**

1. foot   2. hook   3. wood

4. brook   5. hood   6. crook

7. cook

D **Write the spelling words in alphabetical order.**

1. brook   2. cook   3. crook   4. foot

5. hood   6. hook   7. stood   8. wood

DAY 3

Words with *oo*

foot	wood	stood	crook
hook	brook	hood	cook

A **Use the correct spelling words to complete the story.**

I went fishing last week with my friend. We _____stood_____ beside a little _____brook_____ to catch the fish. We were going to _____cook_____ what we caught.

I cast out my line and caught a big fish. I was pulling the _____hook_____ out of the fish's mouth when my _____foot_____ slipped. The fish flew out of my hand and into the water. There went our supper!

B **Write a spelling word under each picture.**

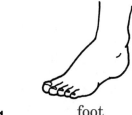 

1. _____foot_____   2. _____hook_____   3. _____cook_____

C **Fill in each blank with a spelling word.**

1. Write the words that end with *ook*.

_____hook_____   _____crook_____

_____brook_____   _____cook_____

2. Write the words that end with *ood*.

_____wood_____   _____stood_____   _____hood_____

3. Write the word that ends with a *t*.

_____foot_____

Name _____

Words with *oo*

foot	wood	stood	crook
hook	brook	hood	cook

A Find each hidden word from the list.

foot	brook	crook	proud
hook	stood	cook	ground
wood	hood	cloud	pound

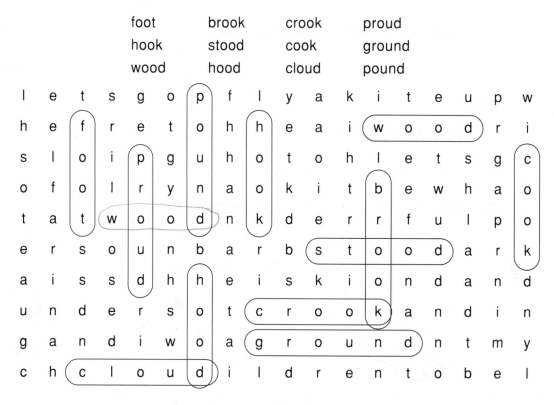

B Use each spelling word in a sentence.

hook _____

wood _____

brook _____

C Change one letter in each spelling word to make a new word.

_____book_____ **1.** Change "brook" to something you read.

_____hoot_____ **2.** Change "foot" to what an owl says.

_____cook_____ **3.** Change "hook" to the name of a person who fixes food.

28

DAY 1

Words with *oo*

food	bloom	booth	goose
noon	loose	tooth	proof

A Fill in each blank with a spelling word.

1. The flowers are ready to _____bloom_____.

2. I am calling you from a phone _____booth_____.

3. I need a belt because my pants are too _____loose_____.

4. The _____food_____ he cooks is really great!

5. The dentist fixed her _____tooth_____.

6. Let's eat lunch today at 12 _____noon_____.

7. There is _____proof_____ that Earth is round.

8. A _____goose_____ looks like a big duck.

B Circle the letters that are the same in all the spelling words.

f(oo)d   n(oo)n   bl(oo)m   l(oo)se   b(oo)th   t(oo)th   g(oo)se   pr(oo)f

C Use the correct spelling words to complete the story.

I sold flowers at our county fair. I rented a _____booth_____ and set up a

sign. At _____noon_____ the crowds arrived. Most of the other booths sold

_____food_____.

A _____goose_____ in the booth next to mine got _____loose_____ and ate

some of my flowers. Then somebody bought the goose. I sold a lot of

flowers, but I used most of my money to buy food at the fair.

Name _____

Words with *oo*

food	bloom	booth	goose
noon	loose	tooth	proof

A Circle the word that is the same as the top one.

food	noon	bloom	loose	booth	tooth	goose	proof
foob	gnoo	dloom	(loose)	booht	booth	(goose)	groof
feed	nune	bloow	leese	dooth	(tooth)	joose	proot
tood	(noon)	(bloom)	loase	(booth)	footh	geese	(proof)
(food)	soon	bleem	looes	beeth	thoot	gooes	pnoof

B Write the spelling words in alphabetical order.

1. _____bloom_____ 2. _____booth_____ 3. _____food_____ 4. _____goose_____

5. _____loose_____ 6. _____noon_____ 7. _____proof_____ 8. _____tooth_____

C Write each spelling word beside its clue.

_____goose_____ **1.** an animal that makes a honking sound

_____food_____ **2.** what we eat to stay alive

_____booth_____ **3.** the place where people vote

_____tooth_____ **4.** one of the things you chew with

_____noon_____ **5.** lunchtime

_____bloom_____ **6.** the flower on a plant

_____proof_____ **7.** what you use to prove something

_____loose_____ **8.** not tight

Words with *oo*

food	bloom	booth	goose
noon	loose	tooth	proof

A Find the missing letters. Then write the word.

1. <u>n</u> <u>o</u> o n   <u>noon</u>

2. b l <u>o</u> <u>o</u> <u>m</u>   <u>bloom</u>

B Use spelling words to complete the puzzle.

Across

2. Flowers ____ in spring.

4. The boy lost his first ___.

6. not tight

7. what we eat

Down

1. lunchtime

2. a stall at a fair

3. It looks like a duck.

5. evidence

Name _____

Lesson 7

Words with *oo*

| food | bloom | booth | goose |
| noon | loose | tooth | proof |

A Fill in the boxes with the correct spelling words.

1. | l | o | o | s | e |

2. | t | o | o | t | h |

3. | p | r | o | o | f |

4. | g | o | o | s | e |

5. | b | o | o | t | h |

6. | b | l | o | o | m |

7. | n | o | o | n |

8. | f | o | o | d |

B Write a spelling word under each picture.

1. ___tooth___ 2. ___goose___ 3. ___bloom___

C Use each spelling word in a sentence.

food _____

noon _____

bloom _____

loose _____

booth _____

tooth _____

goose _____

proof _____

Lesson 8

DAY 1

Words with *ie*

thief	niece	field	brief
chief	piece	shield	yield

A **Fill in each blank with a spelling word.**

1. Who is the _____chief_____ of police?

2. Your brother's daughter is your _____niece_____.

3. An umbrella will _____shield_____ you from the rain.

4. A farmer plants crops in a _____field_____.

5. I would love a _____piece_____ of cake.

6. The _____thief_____ ran off with my purse.

7. The yellow, three-sided road sign means to _____yield_____.

8. She told us a _____brief_____ story, and then we left early.

B **Write the spelling word that rhymes with the word pair.**

1. shield   yield   _____field_____

2. chief   brief   _____thief_____

3. geese   piece   _____niece_____

C **Write the spelling words that name things you can touch.**

1. _____thief_____   2. _____niece_____   3. _____field_____

4. _____chief_____   5. _____piece_____   6. _____shield_____

D **Complete each sentence.**

1. I saw a <u>field</u> of _____.

2. May I have a <u>piece</u> of _____?

Name _____

33

Lesson 8

DAY 2

Words with *ie*

thief	niece	field	brief
chief	piece	shield	yield

A Find the missing letters. Then write the word.

1. s <u>h</u> <u>i</u> <u>e</u> l <u>d</u>   <u>shield</u>

2. y <u>i</u> <u>e</u> <u>l</u> d   <u>yield</u>

3. t <u>h</u> i <u>e</u> <u>f</u>   <u>thief</u>

B Write each spelling word beside its clue.

<u>field</u>   **1.** an open land area often used for planting crops

<u>chief</u>   **2.** the leader of a group or tribe

<u>yield</u>   **3.** a sign that means slow down and let others go first

<u>thief</u>   **4.** a person who steals

<u>niece</u>   **5.** your sister's daughter

<u>piece</u>   **6.** a part or a bit of something

<u>brief</u>   **7.** something that is short or doesn't take much time

<u>shield</u>   **8.** something that protects you

C Circle the letters that are the same in all the spelling words.

th(ie)f   ch(ie)f   n(ie)ce   p(ie)ce   f(ie)ld   sh(ie)ld   br(ie)f   y(ie)ld

Lesson 8 — Words with *ie*

thief	niece	field	brief
chief	piece	shield	yield

A **Fill in the boxes with the correct spelling words.**

1. p i e c e

2. b r i e f

3. y i e l d

4. s h i e l d

5. n i e c e

6. f i e l d

B **One word is wrong in each sentence. Circle the wrong word. Then fill in the blank with a spelling word that makes sense.**

1. I planted corn in the (toaster,) and it grew very well. _field_

2. My brother's little girl is my (aunt.) _niece_

3. The police chased the (chair) down the street. _thief_

4. Each person got a (bucket) of cake at the party. _piece_

5. The knights in the castle had a (feather) to protect them from flying arrows. _shield_

6. When you see the word ("store,") you must slow down and let others go first. _yield_

7. The leader of a company is sometimes called its (flower.) _chief_

8. If you want people to listen to your speech, it should be (boring) and to the point. _brief_

C **Write the spelling words that end with a silent letter.**

niece   _piece_

Name _____

Words with *ie*

thief	niece	field	brief
chief	piece	shield	yield

A   **Use the correct spelling words to complete the story.**

My ____niece____ and I were out for a ride in my car. Suddenly, I saw

lights flash behind me. The ____chief____ of police made us stop by the

side of the road.

Did I run through a ____yield____ sign, or did the chief think I was a

____thief____? I was afraid I would get a ticket and have to pay a fine.

But the chief was very nice. He said a ____piece____ of my taillight was

broken. I thanked him and went on my way.

B   **Write the spelling words in alphabetical order.**

1. ____brief____ 2. ____chief____ 3. ____field____ 4. ____niece____

5. ____piece____ 6. ____shield____ 7. ____thief____ 8. ____yield____

C   **Use each spelling word in a sentence.**

niece _____

field _____

brief _____

yield _____

shield _____

piece _____

chief _____

thief _____

Homonyms

road	pail	ate	see
rode	pale	eight	sea

A **Fill in each blank with a spelling word.**

1. A ____pail____ is a bucket in which you carry water.

2. ____See____ the horse running down the street!

3. You look as ____pale____ as a ghost.

4. We stopped for a picnic on the side of the ____road____.

5. They ____rode____ horses all day at the ranch.

6. We ____ate____ too much watermelon at the party.

7. The huge aquarium had many ____sea____ animals.

8. ____Eight____ people is too many to fit into a car.

B **Circle the correct answer to complete the sentence.**

1. "Pail" and "pale" have different meanings, but they _____.

   (sound the same)   look the same   feel the same

2. Words that sound the same but are not spelled the same are _____.

   synonyms   (homonyms)   antonyms

3. The words in this lesson are called _____.

   synonyms   (homonyms)   antonyms

4. It is _____ that this lesson has four homonym pairs.

   (true)   false

C **Find the missing letters. Then write the word.**

1. p a _l_ e   ____pale____

2. e i _g_ _h_ _t_   ____eight____

Name _____

Homonyms

| road | pail | ate | see |
| rode | pale | eight | sea |

A Write the spelling words that rhyme with the word pair.

1. load   toad   _____ rode, road _____

2. sail   tail   _____ pail, pale _____

3. date   bait   _____ ate, eight _____

4. be   fee   _____ see, sea _____

5. fail   sail   _____ pail, pale _____

6. sewed   code   _____ road, rode _____

7. rate   late   _____ ate, eight _____

B Write a spelling word under each picture.

 **8**

1. _____ pail _____   2. _____ eight _____   3. _____ road _____

C Write the spelling words in alphabetical order.

1. _____ ate _____   2. _____ eight _____   3. _____ pail _____   4. _____ pale _____

5. _____ road _____   6. _____ rode _____   7. _____ sea _____   8. _____ see _____

D Write the spelling words that name things you can touch.

1. _____ road _____   2. _____ pail _____   3. _____ sea _____

DAY 3

Homonyms

road	pail	ate	see
rode	pale	eight	sea

A **Use the correct spelling words to complete the story.**

My friends and I spent a week by the ___sea___. We had a contest

to ___see___ who could build the best sand castle. We decided to start

at ___eight___ o'clock in the morning.

On the day of the contest, I woke up early. I ___ate___ breakfast

and found a ___pail___ to put the sand in. I ___rode___ my bike down

to the shore.

We started building castles. By ten o'clock, we were finished. I had worked

hard on my castle, and I was very tired. The sun was already turning my

___pale___ face red.

I felt much better after the judges voted and named the winner. My sand

castle won first prize!

B **Write each spelling word beside its clue.**

___eight___	**1.** the number after seven
___sea___	**2.** the ocean
___see___	**3.** what you do with your eyes
___pale___	**4.** not having much color
___pail___	**5.** a bucket for carrying water
___road___	**6.** what cars travel on

Name _____

Lesson 9   Homonyms

road	pail	ate	see
rode	pale	eight	sea

A Fill in the boxes with the correct spelling words.

1. p a i l

2. a t e

3. see — s e a

4. e i g h t

5. pale — r o d e

6. r o a d

B Use spelling words to complete the puzzle.

Across

2. the ocean

4. what your eyes do

6. I ___ a horse at the ranch.

7. a bucket

Down

1. light in color

3. I ___ hot dogs for dinner last night.

5. comes after seven

6. a street

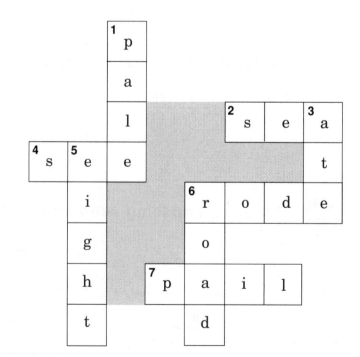

Words with *ea*

| breath | thread | feather | weather |
| spread | ready | heavy | leather |

A **Fill in each blank with a spelling word.**

1. Let's _____ spread _____ out the food on the picnic table.

2. This chair is very _____ heavy _____.

3. A _____ feather _____ fell off the duck's back.

4. Can you _____ thread _____ the needle without your glasses?

5. Are you _____ ready _____ to go to the store?

6. I was out of _____ breath _____ at the end of the race.

7. The _____ weather _____ will be hot and sunny today.

8. Do you like this _____ leather _____ belt?

B **Write a spelling word under each picture.**

1. _____ thread _____ 2. _____ feather _____ 3. _____ spread _____

C **Circle the letters that are the same in all the spelling words.**

br(ea)th   spr(ea)d   thr(ea)d   r(ea)dy   f(ea)ther   h(ea)vy   w(ea)ther   l(ea)ther

D **Write the spelling words that name things you can touch.**

1. _____ thread _____ 2. _____ feather _____ 3. _____ leather _____

Name _____

Words with *ea*

breath	thread	feather	weather
spread	ready	heavy	leather

A Fill in the boxes with the correct spelling words.

1. r e a d y

2. h e a v y

3. f e a t h e r

4. s p r e a d

5. b r e a t h

6. w e a t h e r

7. t h r e a d

8. l e a t h e r

B Write each spelling word beside its clue.

_____leather_____ **1.** what most shoes are made of

_____weather_____ **2.** can be rainy, sunny, cloudy, stormy, or cold

_____spread_____ **3.** how you put butter on bread

_____thread_____ **4.** what you use with a needle to sew clothes

_____breath_____ **5.** the air you breathe in or out

_____feather_____ **6.** one of what a chicken has instead of fur

C Write the spelling words in alphabetical order.

1. _____breath_____   2. _____feather_____   3. _____heavy_____

4. _____leather_____   5. _____ready_____   6. _____spread_____

7. _____thread_____   8. _____weather_____

Words with *ea*

breath	thread	feather	weather
spread	ready	heavy	leather

A **Find each hidden word from the list.**

breath	ready	weather	trail
spread	feather	leather	plain
thread	heavy	mail	brain

```
j  a  s  o  n  i  f  e  a  t  h  e  r  s  l  m  y  s
s  o  n  h  r  y  a  n  s  f  r  i  t  e  e  n  d  p
t  h  e  e  y  p  b  r  a  i  n  l  r  a  a  y  t  r
o  g  e  a  t  h  e  r  i  n  t  h  a  e  t  s  w  e
t  i  m  v  m  i  b  r  e  a  t  h  i  g  h  p  o  a
h  o  l  y  t  h  e  y  l  i  k  e  l  t  e  o  l  d
r  i  s  t  e  n  t  o  s  t  o  r  i  e  r  s  t  h
e  a  p  l  a  i  n  w  e  a  t  h  e  r  t  j  a  s
a  o  n  s  m  o  m  t  a  m  m  y  r  e  a  d  s  t
d  o  t  h  e  m  a  i  l  m  s  h  r  e  a  d  y  e
```

B **Use the correct spelling words to complete the story.**

I helped my uncle make a cement porch. It wasn't as hard as I thought it would be. When the ____weather____ was dry and sunny, we marked off a place for the porch. Then we got the ground ____ready____.

My uncle mixed the cement. Then we poured it in the place we had marked. We had to work fast before the cement became hard. We ____spread____ it with a tool called a trowel. By the next day, the porch was dry. My uncle and I were proud of the porch we made.

Name _____

Words with *ea*

breath	thread	feather	weather
spread	ready	heavy	leather

A Find the missing letters. Then write the word.

1. s p _r_ _e_ _a_ d   spread

2. b r _e_ _a_ _t_ h   breath

3. f _e_ _a_ t h _e_ r   feather

B Use each spelling word in a sentence.

breath _____

spread _____

thread _____

ready _____

feather _____

heavy _____

weather _____

leather _____

C One word is wrong in each sentence. Circle the wrong word. Then fill in the blank with a spelling word that makes sense.

1. The sofa is very (green) to pick up.   heavy

2. I sew with a needle and (rope.)   thread

3. She (threw) the jelly on the toast.   spread

4. We found a duck's (tail) near the pond.   feather

5. My belt is made of (sand.)   leather

foot	stood	food	booth	thief
hook	hood	noon	tooth	chief
wood	crook	bloom	goose	niece
brook	cook	loose	proof	piece

A **Write a spelling word under each picture.**

1. _____foot_____   2. _____tooth_____   3. _____goose_____

B **Fill in each blank with a spelling word.**

1. My rat got out of its cage, and now it's _____loose_____!

2. Let's eat lunch at 12 _____noon_____.

3. I will not pull a _____hook_____ out of a fish's mouth.

4. A person that steals is a _____thief_____.

5. I need _____proof_____ that you are old enough to drive.

6. May I have a _____piece_____ of your birthday cake?

7. We need more _____wood_____ for our fire.

8. My _____niece_____ and nephew are coming to visit me.

9. That jacket also has a _____hood_____.

10. I'm helping my mom make the _____food_____ for dinner tonight.

11. We are setting up a _____booth_____ at our county fair.

12. The flowers will _____bloom_____ in spring.

Name _____

field	road	ate	breath	feather
shield	rode	eight	spread	heavy
brief	pail	see	thread	weather
yield	pale	sea	ready	leather

C **Write the spelling words that rhyme with the word pair.**

1. load   mode   rode, road

2. tea   free   sea, see

3. late   rate   ate, eight

4. mail   tail   pail, pale

5. thief   chief   brief

D **Use the correct spelling words to complete the story.**

I was working outside in a large _____field_____ with several of my friends. We were picking strawberries. Suddenly the _____weather_____ started to change. Clouds were forming and a _____heavy_____ rain began to fall. I _____spread_____ my coat across as many of my friends as I could, and we got _____ready_____ to run. The coat was our only _____shield_____ against the rain and hail. We picked up our buckets that were filled to the top with strawberries. The buckets were so full that it was difficult to carry them.

We ran across the road and jumped in our car. It was hard for us to catch our _____breath_____ because we were so tired and wet. It was hard to see through the rain, so we drove home slowly. We remember that day every time we eat strawberries.

Words with *ear*

heard	earn	earth	yearn
learn	pearl	search	early

A Fill in each blank with a spelling word.

1. You have to wake up _____early_____ to go to school on time.

2. The diver found a _____pearl_____ in the oyster.

3. Dirt is also called _____earth_____.

4. I _____yearn_____ to win first place.

5. We had to _____search_____ for our lost kitten.

6. How much money do you _____earn_____ on your paper route?

7. I _____heard_____ that story when I was a child.

8. What did you _____learn_____ in school today?

B Circle the letters that are the same in all the spelling words.

hd   ln   n   pl   th   sch   yn   ly

C Write the spelling words that rhyme with the word pair.

1. bird   third   _____heard_____

2. curl   girl   _____pearl_____

3. church   perch   _____search_____

4. burn   fern   ___learn, earn, yearn___

5. stern   earn   ___yearn, learn___

6. curly   surly   _____early_____

7. birth   worth   _____earth_____

Name _____

DAY 2

Words with *ear*

heard	earn	earth	yearn
learn	pearl	search	early

A Put an *X* on the word that is <u>not</u> the same.

1. heard	heard	ha~~r~~d	heard	heard
2. learn	le~~a~~n	learn	learn	learn
3. earn	earn	earn	ear~~n~~	earn
4. pearl	qearl	pearl	pearl	pearl
5. earth	earth	ear~~h~~t	earth	earth
6. search	sa~~r~~ch	search	search	search
7. yearn	yearn	ya~~r~~n	yearn	yearn

B Write a spelling word under each picture.

1. _____heard_____ **2.** _____pearl_____ **3.** _____earth_____

C Write the spelling words that name things you <u>cannot</u> touch.

1. _____heard_____ **2.** _____earn_____ **3.** _____learn_____

4. _____search_____ **5.** _____early_____ **6.** _____yearn_____

D Write the spelling words in alphabetical order.

1. _____early_____ **2.** _____earn_____ **3.** _____earth_____ **4.** _____heard_____

5. _____learn_____ **6.** _____pearl_____ **7.** _____search_____ **8.** _____yearn_____

Words with *ear*

heard	earn	earth	yearn
learn	pearl	search	early

A **Use the correct spelling words to complete the story.**

Have you _____heard_____ how an oyster makes a _____pearl_____?

An oyster is an animal that lives in the ocean. It starts with an accident

_____early_____ in an oyster's life. A bit of sand gets in the oyster's shell. The

lining of the shell starts to cover the piece of sand. Layers of the shell lining

build up over the years. Finally, a pearl is formed.

You have to look in many oysters to find just one pearl. But the

_____search_____ is worth it. A perfect, round pearl is worth a lot of money.

People have studied oysters to _____learn_____ how to get them to make

pearls. A piece of sand or shell can be put into young oysters. Then the

oysters are kept in special cages. After a few years, about one out of twenty

oysters will have a beautiful pearl inside its shell.

B **Fill in the boxes with the correct spelling words.**

1. | e | a | r | n |

2. | s | e | a | r | c | h |

3. | e | a | r | t | h |

4. | y | e | a | r | n |

5. | p | e | a | r | l |

6. | h | e | a | r | d |

7. | l | e | a | r | n |

8. | e | a | r | l | y |

Name _____

DAY 4

Words with *ear*

heard	earn	earth	yearn
learn	pearl	search	early

A Find the missing letters. Then write the word.

1. <u>h</u> e a r d   <u>   heard   </u>

2. <u>e</u> <u>a</u> <u>r</u> t h   <u>   earth   </u>

B Write each spelling word beside its clue.

<u>   learn   </u>   **1.** to get to know something by study or practice

<u>   earn   </u>   **2.** to deserve or win

<u>   pearl   </u>   **3.** a white jewel formed in oysters

<u>   yearn   </u>   **4.** to want something very much

<u>   search   </u>   **5.** to look for something

<u>   earth   </u>   **6.** dirt or soil

C Use each spelling word in a sentence.

heard   _____

learn   _____

earn   _____

pearl   _____

earth   _____

search   _____

yearn   _____

early   _____

Words with -*y*

cry	dry	fly	spy
fry	shy	sky	pry

A Fill in each blank with a spelling word.

1. The _____sky_____ is very blue today.

2. I need to _____dry_____ my wet clothes.

3. Let's _____fry_____ the fish over the campfire.

4. I began to _____cry_____ when I heard the bad news.

5. The puppy was so _____shy_____ that it hid behind the sofa.

6. I'm trying to swat that _____fly_____ away from me!

7. She had to _____pry_____ the lid off the jar.

8. You should not _____spy_____ on your friends.

B Answer the questions with spelling words.

1. Which words end with *ry*?

    ___cry___   ___dry___   ___fry___   ___pry___

2. Which words begin with *s*?

    ___shy___   ___sky___   ___spy___

3. Which words do these words come from?

pries	___pry___	spies	___spy___
dries	___dry___	cries	___cry___
fries	___fry___	flies	___fly___

C Circle the letter that is the same in all the spelling words.

cr(y)   fr(y)   dr(y)   sh(y)   fl(y)   sk(y)   sp(y)   pr(y)

Name _____

Lesson 12

DAY
2

Words with -*y*

cry	dry	fly	spy
fry	shy	sky	pry

A **Put an *X* on the word that is <u>not</u> the same.**

1.	cry	cry	c~~ry~~	cry	cry
2.	fry	f~~ry~~	fry	fry	fry
3.	dry	dry	dry	dry	~~dry~~
4.	shy	shy	s~~hy~~	shy	shy
5.	fly	~~fly~~	fly	fly	fly

B **Fill in the boxes with the correct spelling words.**

1. f l y

2. s p y

3. p r y

4. s h y

5. fry / d r y

6. s k y

C **Use each spelling word in a sentence.**

cry _____

fry _____

dry _____

shy _____

fly _____

sky _____

spy _____

pry _____

52

Lesson 12

Words with -*y*

cry	dry	fly	spy
fry	shy	sky	pry

A   **Use the correct spelling words to complete the story.**

I love good _____spy_____ movies. They keep you on the edge of

your seat.

My favorite actor played a spy named James Bond. He had special

cars that could do everything but _____fly_____. Even his watch was full

of tricks.

In one movie, a man puts a deadly spider in James Bond's bed. You see the

spider crawl across Bond's chest. Whenever I see this part, I _____cry_____

out, "Don't move!" But things always turn out all right for him.

I'd love to meet this actor in person someday. But I'm sure I'd be too

_____shy_____ to even speak to him.

B   **Write the spelling words in alphabetical order.**

1. ____cry____   2. ____dry____   3. ____fly____   4. ____fry____

5. ____pry____   6. ____shy____   7. ____sky____   8. ____spy____

C   **Complete each sentence. Use a dictionary if you need to.**

1. "Cry" means _____.

2. "Spy" means _____.

3. "Shy" means _____.

4. "Pry" means _____.

Name _____

Lesson 12

DAY 4

Words with -*y*

cry	dry	fly	spy
fry	shy	sky	pry

A Write the spelling word that matches its antonym (opposite).

1. ground ____sky____

2. outgoing ____shy____

3. laugh ____cry____

4. wet ____dry____

B Add *ing* to the spelling words below. Then write sentences using the new words.

cry _*crying*_ _*The baby is crying.*_

dry ____drying____ _____

fly ____flying____ _____

spy ____spying____ _____

fry ____frying____ _____

pry ____prying____ _____

C Fill in each blank with a spelling word.

1. Write the word that belongs with cooking.

____fry____

2. Write the word that tells what birds do.

____fly____

3. Write the word that tells where clouds float.

____sky____

Lesson 13   Homonyms

to	for	bear	flour
two	four	bare	flower

A **Fill in each blank with a spelling word.**

1. She walked outside in her _____bare_____ feet.

2. This cake calls for sifted _____flour_____.

3. Please open the door _____for_____ me.

4. Half of a month is about _____two_____ weeks.

5. Will you go with me _____to_____ the party?

6. Two, _____four_____ six, eight! Who do we appreciate?

7. Did you see that big _____bear_____ in the park?

8. His mother wore a pretty _____flower_____ on her blouse.

B **Fill in each blank with a spelling word.**

1. Write the words that have both *a* and *e* in them.

   _____bare_____   _____bear_____

2. Write the shortest word. _____to_____

3. Write the longest word. _____flower_____

4. Write the words that are numbers.

   _____two_____   _____four_____

C **Write a spelling word under each picture.**

  **4**

1. _____bear_____   2. _____flower_____   3. _____four_____

Name _____

Lesson 13 Homonyms

| to | for | bear | flour |
| two | four | bare | flower |

A Fill in the boxes with the correct spelling words.

1. bear/bare
   | f | o | u | r |

2. four/bare
   | b | e | a | r |

3. | f | l | o | u | r |

4. for
   | t | w | o |

5. | t | o |

6. | f | l | o | w | e | r |

B Circle the correct answer to complete the sentence.

1. The four pairs of words in this lesson are _____.

   synonyms   (homonyms)   antonyms

2. The word _____ has as many letters as the number it is.

   for   (four)

3. One of the *b* words is an animal. It is _____.

   (bear)   bare

4. One of the words is visited by bees. It is _____.

   flour   (flower)

5. It is _____ that two of the words are living things.

   (true)   false

C Write the spelling words in alphabetical order.

1. ___bare___ 2. ___bear___ 3. ___flour___ 4. ___flower___

5. ___for___ 6. ___four___ 7. ___to___ 8. ___two___

Homonyms

DAY 3

to	for	bear	flour
two	four	bare	flower

A ### Find each hidden word from the list.

to	four	flour	coast
two	bear	flower	load
for	bare	toast	road

```
p  o  d  f  b  o  u  r  r  h  f  a  s  f  o  u  r
j  u  d  y  a  a  n  d  o  d  l  o  a  d  e  n  i
s  e  a  n  r  d  b  a  a  r  o  b  a  r  a  a  n
d  b  t  r  e  b  a  r  d  a  u  a  n  c  d  a  t
f  l  s  o  p  f  h  e  r  n  r  e  s  o  h  e  w
o  y  h  a  v  l  e  f  i  f  t  h  a  a  d  d  o
r  s  i  x  t  o  a  s  t  t  h  g  r  s  a  d  e
r  s  a  n  d  w  i  l  i  k  e  t  h  t  e  m  a
l  l  v  e  r  e  y  m  u  c  h  t  h  e  y  d  o
l  o  t  s  o  r  f  t  h  g  o  o  b  e  a  r  d
```

B ### Write each spelling word beside its clue.

__flour__ **1.** this is used to make bread

__bear__ **2.** an animal with thick fur, short legs, and sharp claws

__four__ **3.** the number after three

__bare__ **4.** not covered

__two__ **5.** the number after one

__flower__ **6.** the blossom of a plant

Name _____

DAY 4

Homonyms

to	for	bear	flour
two	four	bare	flower

A **Use the correct spelling words to complete the story.**

We were on a campout. It was my turn _____to_____ go into town for

food. The store was just _____two_____ miles from camp, so I went on foot.

On the way, I stopped to admire a _____flower_____. Right beside the

flowers were some paw prints. I bent down to study the prints. I'd seen them

before in a book.

They looked like _____bear_____ tracks. Bears! I ran _____for_____ my

life back to camp.

B **Use each spelling word in a sentence.**

to _____

two _____

for _____

four _____

bear _____

bare _____

flour _____

flower _____

C **Find the missing letters. Then write the word.**

1. f _l_ _o_ _w_ e r   _____flower_____

2. b _e_ _a_ r   _____bear_____

DAY 1

Words with *eigh*

sleigh	weigh	neighbor	eighty
freight	weight	neigh	freighter

A Fill in each blank with a spelling word.

1. A ____freighter____ is a ship that carries cargo.

2. Let's ride a ____sleigh____ through the snow.

3. The doctor will ____weigh____ you on the scale.

4. The ____freight____ on the truck was fruits and vegetables.

5. The hog's ____weight____ was 300 pounds.

6. My ____neighbor____ next door has a very nice yard.

7. The horse gave a loud ____neigh____ and threw back its head.

8. There were ____eighty____ people on the jet plane.

B Circle the letters that are the same in all the spelling words.

sl(eigh)   fr(eigh)t   w(eigh)   w(eigh)t   n(eigh)bor   n(eigh)   (eigh)ty   fr(eigh)ter

C Write the spelling words that rhyme with the word pair.

1. day   ray   ____sleigh, weigh, neigh____

2. date   rate   ____freight, weight____

D One word is wrong in each sentence. Circle the wrong word. Then fill in the blank with a spelling word that makes sense.

1. She is my next-door (tractor.)   ____neighbor____

2. How much does the box (height?)   ____weigh____

3. It's fun to ride a (snake) in the snow.   ____sleigh____

Name _____

59

DAY 2

Words with *eigh*

sleigh	weigh	neighbor	eighty
freight	weight	neigh	freighter

A Find each hidden word from the list.

sleigh	weight	eighty	shade
freight	neighbor	freighter	flake
weigh	neigh	blade	snake

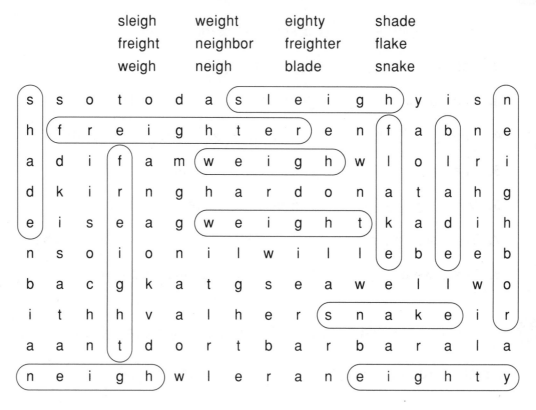

B Write a spelling word under each picture.

1. _____eighty_____ 2. _____sleigh_____ 3. _____freighter_____

C Write the spelling words in alphabetical order.

1. ____eighty____ 2. ____freight____ 3. ____freighter____ 4. ____neigh____

5. ____neighbor____ 6. ____sleigh____ 7. ____weigh____ 8. ____weight____

Words with *eigh*

sleigh	weigh	neighbor	eighty
freight	weight	neigh	freighter

A Use the correct spelling words to complete the story.

I had a _____neighbor_____ once who was almost _____eighty_____ years

old. He liked to tell me stories. When he was a young man, he used to work

on a _____freighter_____. A freighter is a ship that carries freight. His job was

to _____weigh_____ the freight as it was loaded on the ship. Sometimes

the freight would weigh a lot. Then he would have to figure out how much to

charge the owners of the freight.

B Write each spelling word beside its clue.

_____freight_____ **1.** goods that are carried by land, sea, or air

_____neighbor_____ **2.** someone who lives close to you

_____weight_____ **3.** the amount that something weighs

_____neigh_____ **4.** the sound a horse makes

_____freighter_____ **5.** a ship carrying cargo

_____weigh_____ **6.** what you do to find the weight of something

_____sleigh_____ **7.** something to ride in through the snow

_____eighty_____ **8.** the number after 79

C Write the spelling words that name things you can touch.

1. _____sleigh_____ **2.** _____neighbor_____ **3.** _____freight_____

4. _____freighter_____

Name _____

Words with *eigh*

sleigh	weigh	neighbor	eighty
freight	weight	neigh	freighter

A Put an *X* on the word that is <u>not</u> the same.

1.	sleigh	sleigh	~~sleihg~~	sleigh	sleigh
2.	freight	freight	freight	~~freighf~~	freight
3.	weigh	~~wiegh~~	weigh	weigh	weigh
4.	weight	weight	weight	weight	~~weighf~~
5.	neighbor	neighbor	~~neighdor~~	neighbor	neighbor
6.	neigh	neigh	~~neijh~~	neigh	neigh
7.	eighty	~~eihgty~~	eighty	eighty	eighty

B Circle the correct answer that matches its clue.

1. Seventy-nine comes before this.

    eight   (eighty)

2. Most trucks on the road carry this.

    sleigh   (freight)   neighbor

3. This is a person that lives close to you.

    freight   (neighbor)   sleigh

4. This is something that you ride in.

    neigh   (sleigh)   weigh

5. You find this out when you read a scale.

    (weight)   freight   eight

6. This is a ship that carries cargo.

    freight   sleigh   (freighter)

Lesson 15

Words with *kn-*

kneel	knife	knot	knight
knock	knit	knob	knack

A **Fill in each blank with a spelling word.**

1. The door _____knob_____ fell off when I touched it.

2. Did you _____knit_____ that pretty sweater?

3. We learned how to tie a _____knot_____ with a rope.

4. She has a _____knack_____ for saying the right thing.

5. A _____knight_____ was a soldier in King Arthur's court.

6. The new _____knife_____ is very sharp.

7. Please _____knock_____ before you come in my room.

8. You have to _____kneel_____ down to work in the garden.

B **Circle the letters that are the same in all the spelling words.**

(kn)eel (kn)ock (kn)ife (kn)it (kn)ot (kn)ob (kn)ight (kn)ack

C **Write the spelling word that rhymes with the word pair.**

1. sock   rock   _____knock_____

2. fit   kit   _____knit_____

3. bite   kite   _____knight_____

4. cot   lot   _____knot_____

5. wife   life   _____knife_____

6. feel   peel   _____kneel_____

7. cob   sob   _____knob_____

8. sack   pack   _____knack_____

Name _____

Words with *kn-*

kneel	knife	knot	knight
knock	knit	knob	knack

A Put an *X* on the word that is <u>not</u> the same.

1.	kneel	kne̶l̶l̶	kneel	kneel	kneel
2.	knock	knock	knock	knock	kne̶c̶k
3.	knife	knife	kni̶t̶e̶	knife	knife
4.	knit	knit	knit	kni̶t̶	knit
5.	knot	kno̶f̶	knot	knot	knot
6.	knob	kno̶d̶	knob	knob	knob
7.	knight	knight	knighf̶	knight	knight
8.	knack	knack	knack	kank̶	knack

B Write each spelling word beside its clue.

Word	Clue
knife	**1.** a kitchen tool used for cutting
knob	**2.** a round handle for opening a door
knack	**3.** a talent for doing something
knight	**4.** a soldier who fought for a king or queen
knot	**5.** a fastening or a tangle
knock	**6.** to hit or rap
kneel	**7.** to rest on your knees
knit	**8.** to loop yarn together for clothes

C Write the spelling words that name things you can touch.

1. knife   2. knot   3. knight   4. knob

Lesson 15   # Words with *kn-*

kneel	**knife**	**knot**	**knight**
knock	**knit**	**knob**	**knack**

A **Use the correct spelling words to complete the story.**

Have you heard this fairy tale? In the woods lived a man who had a

___knack___ for solving problems. One day there was a ___knock___

at the man's door. The king had come to ask the man to help his daughter, the

princess. Someone had put a spell on the princess and turned her into a cat.

The man went back to the castle with the king. He asked to see the cat.

Then he pulled a ___knife___ out of his pocket. He cut off a bit of the

cat's hair. He spoke some words of magic. The cat turned back into the

princess.

The king was very happy. He had the man ___kneel___ before him

and made him a ___knight___ of the royal court.

B **Write a spelling word under each picture.**

1. ___knock___   2. ___knot___   3. ___knight___

C **Fill in the boxes with the correct spelling words.**

1.  knot
k	n	o	b

2. | k | n | i | g | h | t |
   |---|---|---|---|---|---|

3. | k | n | e | e | l |
   |---|---|---|---|---|
   knock/knack

4. | k | n | i | t |
   |---|---|---|---|

5. | k | n | o | c | k |
   |---|---|---|---|---|
   kneel/knack

6. | k | n | i | f | e |
   |---|---|---|---|---|

Name _____

DAY
4

Words with *kn-*

kneel	knife	knot	knight
knock	knit	knob	knack

A Find the missing letters. Then write the word.

1. k <u>n</u> <u>i</u> <u>g</u> <u>h</u> t   <u>knight</u>

2. k <u>n</u> <u>i</u> <u>f</u> e   <u>knife</u>

B Match each spelling word with a related word.

<u>h</u>   **1.** kneel   **a.** fork

<u>d</u>   **2.** knock   **b.** door

<u>a</u>   **3.** knife   **c.** talent

<u>f</u>   **4.** knit   **d.** rap

<u>g</u>   **5.** knot   **e.** soldier

<u>b</u>   **6.** knob   **f.** sweater

<u>e</u>   **7.** knight   **g.** rope

<u>c</u>   **8.** knack   **h.** bend

C Answer the questions with spelling words.

1. Which words end with *ck*?

   <u>knock</u>   <u>knack</u>

2. Which words have the long *i* sound?

   <u>knife</u>   <u>knight</u>

3. Which words have the short *o* sound?

   <u>knock</u>   <u>knot</u>   <u>knob</u>

4. Which word has the long *e* sound?   <u>kneel</u>

heard	earth	cry	fly	to
learn	search	fry	sky	two
earn	yearn	dry	spy	for
pearl	early	shy	pry	four

A **Write a spelling word under each picture.**

4

1. ___heard___ 2. ___earth___ 3. ___four___

B **Fill in each blank with a spelling word.**

1. Open the oyster shell, and look at the shiny ___pearl___.

2. If you go with us, you'll have to wake up ___early___.

3. I love to ___fly___ my kite with my friends.

4. The ___sky___ is black, and I think it will storm.

5. You need to ___dry___ your clothes before we leave.

6. What did you ___learn___ in class today?

7. Please take care of the baby, or he will ___cry___.

8. I only have ___two___ more hours before my date arrives.

9. We will ___fry___ the eggs in the pan.

10. My sister's new puppy is very quiet and ___shy___.

11. This package is ___for___ your brother.

12. Please give this letter ___to___ her.

Name _____

bear	sleigh	neighbor	kneel	knot
bare	freight	neigh	knock	knob
flour	weigh	eighty	knife	knight
flower	weight	freighter	knit	knack

C **Write the spelling words that rhyme with the word pair.**

1. block   clock   _knock_
2. rare   tear   _bear, bare_
3. weigh   sleigh   _neigh_
4. fit   sit   _knit_
5. feel   seal   _kneel_

D **Use the correct spelling words to complete the story.**

Have you ever heard the story of King Arthur? The story says that he was a King of England, and he had many soldiers. A soldier was called a _knight_. Each knight had a _knack_ or a special way of taking care of the kingdom. Some were good at sword fighting, and some even fought with a long stick called a staff. When the knights put on their armor, the _weight_ of their body would become much heavier. It's amazing that they could even move in their armor!

Although the knights would fight, they were also gentle. They could see the beauty of a fresh _flower_ or have fun with their children as they rode through the snow in a _sleigh_.

Words with *wr-*

wrench	wrist	wreck	wren
wring	wrong	wrestle	wreath

A **Fill in each blank with a spelling word.**

1. She said her messy room was a _____wreck_____.

2. Do you like the _____wreath_____ on our door?

3. The bird singing outside is a _____wren_____.

4. The puppies like to _____wrestle_____ around on the floor.

5. He began to _____wring_____ the water out of his clothes.

6. It is _____wrong_____ to cheat on a test.

7. He broke his _____wrist_____ in the football game.

8. I need a _____wrench_____ to fix the sink.

B **Write the spelling word that rhymes with the word pair.**

1. sing   bring   _____wring_____

2. fist   list   _____wrist_____

3. song   long   _____wrong_____

4. deck   neck   _____wreck_____

5. pen   ten   _____wren_____

6. teeth   sheath   _____wreath_____

C **Write a spelling word under each picture.**

1. _____wren_____   2. _____wreath_____   3. _____wrench_____

Name _____

Words with *wr-*

| wrench | wrist | wreck | wren |
| wring | wrong | wrestle | wreath |

A Circle the letters that are the same in all the spelling words.

(wr)ench (wr)ing (wr)ist (wr)ong (wr)eck (wr)estle (wr)en (wr)eath

B Which letter is silent in all the spelling words? ___w___

C Use spelling words to complete the puzzle.

							¹w
							r
²w	r	e	s	t	l	e
r							c
³w	r	e	n	c	h		k
r		a					
o		t	⁴w	r	i	s	t
n		h	r				
g			e				
	⁵w	r	i	n	g		

Across

2. to struggle with something

3. a tool

4. between the hand and arm

5. to squeeze out or twist

Down

1. Two cars had a ___.

2. a ring of leaves or branches

3. incorrect

4. a songbird

70

DAY
3

Words with *wr-*

wrench	wrist	wreck	wren
wring	wrong	wrestle	wreath

A **Use the correct spelling words to complete the story.**

My friend and I were riding in my car when we saw a line of cars ahead.

We knew something was ____wrong____. All of the cars in our lane began to

slow down. Then we saw a man standing on the side of the road. His car

had broken down. We were so glad it wasn't a bad ____wreck____. We

decided to stop and help him fix his car. I looked in my toolbox and found a

____wrench____ and some other tools. After about twenty minutes, he was able

to start his car. He sure was happy that we stopped to help.

B **Match each spelling word with a related word.**

____e____ **1.** wreath   **a.** crash

____d____ **2.** wren   **b.** watch

____f____ **3.** wrestle   **c.** incorrect

____a____ **4.** wreck   **d.** bird

____c____ **5.** wrong   **e.** decoration

____b____ **6.** wrist   **f.** struggle

____h____ **7.** wring   **g.** tool

____g____ **8.** wrench   **h.** twist

C **Write the spelling words that name things you can touch.**

1. ____wrench____   **2.** ____wrist____

3. ____wren____   **4.** ____wreath____

Name _____

Words with *wr-*

wrench	wrist	wreck	wren
wring	wrong	wrestle	wreath

A Fill in the boxes with the correct spelling words.

1. | w | r | o | n | g |

2. | w | r | e | n |

3. | w | r | e | a | t | h |

4. | w | r | i | s | t |

5. | w | r | e | c | k |

6. | w | r | e | s | t | l | e |

B Write the spelling words in alphabetical order.

1. ___wreath___   2. ___wreck___   3. ___wren___   4. ___wrench___

5. ___wrestle___   6. ___wring___   7. ___wrist___   8. ___wrong___

C Use each spelling word in a sentence.

wrench _____

wring _____

wrist _____

wrong _____

wreck _____

wrestle _____

wren _____

wreath _____

D Find the missing letters. Then write the word.

1. _w_ r _e_ _n_   ___wren___

2. w r _i_ _s_ t   ___wrist___

Contractions with *-n't*

won't	isn't	didn't	hasn't
aren't	doesn't	wasn't	weren't

A **Fill in each blank with a spelling word.**

1. We ___aren't___ ready to leave yet.

2. One twin likes to paint, but the other twin ___doesn't___ .

3. I ___wasn't___ feeling well last week.

4. He ___won't___ be able to go with us.

5. She ___hasn't___ eaten dinner yet.

6. ___Weren't___ you the captain of the team last year?

7. Earth ___isn't___ the largest planet.

8. We almost won today, ___didn't___ we?

B **Circle the letters that are the same in all the spelling words.**

wo(n't)   are(n't)   is(n't)   does(n't)   did(n't)   was(n't)   has(n't)   were(n't)

C **Answer each question.**

1. What word does *n't* stand for? ___not___

2. What are the words in this lesson called?

   homonyms.   (contractions)   compounds.

D **Find the missing letters. Then write the word.**

1. _a_ r e _n_ ' _t_   ___aren't___

2. h _a_ s n ' _t_   ___hasn't___

3. d _o_ e _s_ n ' t   ___doesn't___

Name _____

Lesson 17

Contractions with *-n't*

won't	isn't	didn't	hasn't
aren't	doesn't	wasn't	weren't

A The spelling words in this lesson are called contractions. Match each contraction with its pair of words.

_e_ **1.** isn't   **a.** were not

_f_ **2.** doesn't   **b.** are not

_g_ **3.** hasn't   **c.** will not

_a_ **4.** weren't   **d.** did not

_c_ **5.** won't   **e.** is not

_b_ **6.** aren't   **f.** does not

_d_ **7.** didn't   **g.** has not

B Put an *X* on the word that is <u>not</u> the same.

1. aren't	aren't	aren't	aren't	~~aern't~~
2. didn't	didn't	~~didn't~~	didn't	didn't
3. won't	~~won't~~	won't	won't	won't

C Use spelling words to complete the puzzle.

Across

3. is not

4. were not

5. has not

Down

1. did not

2. are not

Crossword puzzle:

```
                           1
                           d
              2            3
              a            i  s  n  t
              r            d
        4
        w  e  r  e  n  t
              n            t
   5
   h  a  s  n  t
```

74

Contractions with -n't

won't	isn't	didn't	hasn't
aren't	doesn't	wasn't	weren't

A Find each hidden word from the list. The contractions are written without an (').

won't	doesn't	hasn't	state
aren't	didn't	weren't	tame
isn't	wasn't	plate	flame

```
h  s  y  h  e  r  w  a  s  n  t  d  d  n  l  b  h
o  f  a  o  d  o  n  t  t  d  a  h  i  g  i  u  a
m  l  t  o  o  p  i  e  l  i  w  e  d  a  p  t  s
a  a  a  r  e  n  t  r  e  s  h  l  n  n  l  m  n
s  m  o  l  s  e  r  m  f  n  o  p  t  d  a  o  t
w  e  u  s  n  p  e  y  r  t  n  i  a  s  t  s  a
o  v  r  o  t  p  m  w  e  r  e  n  t  p  e  t  l
r  e  s  d  s  e  e  l  i  l  e  n  d  e  n  o  l
s  t  a  t  e  r  m  i  e  w  o  n  t  a  m  e  i
```

B Write the spelling words in alphabetical order.

1. _____aren't_____   2. _____didn't_____   3. _____doesn't_____   4. _____hasn't_____

5. _____isn't_____   6. _____wasn't_____   7. _____weren't_____   8. _____won't_____

C Circle the word that is the same as the top one.

won't	aren't	isn't	doesn't	didn't	wasn't	hasn't	weren't
bon't	(aren't)	isn'f	boesn't	dibn't	(wasn't)	basn't	waren't
(won't)	arem't	sin't	dosen't	(didn't)	wasm't	hasm't	(weren't)
dom't	anen't	(isn't)	daesn't	didn'f	wasn'f	(hasn't)	werem't
don'f	aren'f	ism't	(doesn't)	didm't	wosn't	hosn't	weren'f

Name _____

Lesson 17   Contractions with -n't

won't	isn't	didn't	hasn't
aren't	doesn't	wasn't	weren't

A **Fill in each blank with the correct spelling word.**

1. She ____doesn't____ have to leave early.
   isn't   doesn't

2. They ____weren't____ going to the zoo today.
   weren't   wasn't

3. He ____isn't____ the one who has the ball.
   aren't   isn't

4. It ____hasn't____ been long since they left.
   weren't   hasn't

5. She ____didn't____ know how to use the new computer.
   didn't   hasn't

6. It ____wasn't____ their fault that they were late.
   wasn't   weren't

7. They ____won't____ be attending the party.
   doesn't   won't

8. ____Aren't____ you excited about the trip?
   Isn't   Aren't

B **Use the correct spelling words to complete the story.**

My little brother is six years old. He likes to play baseball. He

____isn't____ a very good player yet, but that ____doesn't____ bother him.

He knows he'll get better with practice.

He is good at throwing the ball. But he ____won't____ run to catch the

ball if it's far away. He also needs to practice batting. He struck out three

times in the last game he played.

I'm going to help him become a better player.

76

DAY 1

Homonyms

blew	hear	sale	knew
blue	here	sail	new

A **Fill in each blank with a spelling word.**

1. The store is having a _____sale_____ on clothes.

2. The truck _____blew_____ a tire and ran off the road.

3. He is _____here_____ today to talk to you.

4. I _____knew_____ her when she was just a little girl.

5. Did you _____hear_____ what he said?

6. The sky is so clear and _____blue_____ today.

7. They will _____sail_____ around the world on a ship.

8. Are you a _____new_____ student, or were you here last year?

B **Circle the correct answer to complete the sentence.**

1. The word pairs in this lesson are _____.

   synonyms   (homonyms)   antonyms

2. "Blue" and "blew" are not spelled alike, but they _____.

   (sound alike)   feel alike   mean the same thing

3. The word that begins with a silent letter is _____.

   sail   blew   here   (knew)

C **Write the spelling words that rhyme with the word pair.**

1. do   flew   _____knew, new, blew, blue_____

2. ear   dear   _____here, hear_____

3. pail   fail   _____sale, sail_____

Name _____

DAY 2

Homonyms

blew	hear	sale	knew
blue	here	sail	new

A Fill in the boxes with the correct spelling words.

1. h e a r

2. s a i l

3. n e w

4. s a l e

5. k n e w

6. b l u e

7. h e r e

8. b l e w

B Write each spelling word beside its clue.

sale	**1.** the act of selling
sail	**2.** a "sheet" for catching wind on a ship
new	**3.** not old
here	**4.** where you are right now
blue	**5.** a color
blew	**6.** what the wind did yesterday
hear	**7.** what you do with your ears
knew	**8.** used to know

C Write the spelling words in alphabetical order.

1. blew   2. blue   3. hear   4. here

5. knew   6. new   7. sail   8. sale

Lesson 18   Homonyms

blew	hear	sale	knew
blue	here	sail	new

A Use the correct spelling words to complete the story.

When I was ten years old, my family moved _____here_____ to be near the

ocean. This was a _____new_____ kind of life for us at first, but we quickly

became used to it. Now I love the water and sun and sand. I can wear shorts

here all the time.

The family next door became our best friends. My mother says she

_____knew_____ right away we'd get along. She was right! We enjoy the same

things. We like to spend time on the beach. In the summer we _____sail_____

our boats together in the bay. On weekends we fish from the pier and cook

our catch outdoors.

We're lucky to live by the ocean. We can go to the beach every day.

B Put an X on the word that is not the same.

1. hear	hare	hear	hear	hear
2. sale	sale	sale	sael	sale
3. knew	knew	knew	knew	know
4. new	now	new	new	new
5. blew	blew	blew	blow	blew
6. blue	blue	bule	blue	blue
7. here	here	here	heer	here
8. sail	sali	sail	sail	sail

Name _____

79

Lesson 18   Homonyms

DAY 4

blew	hear	sale	knew
blue	here	sail	new

A Find the missing letters. Then write the word.

1. b _l_ _u_ e   _blue_

2. _s_ _a_ | e   _sale_

B Answer the questions with spelling words.

1. Which words end with *ew*?

    blew   _knew_   _new_

2. Which word does not have the letter *e* in it?   _sail_

C Use each spelling word in a sentence.

blew _____

blue _____

hear _____

here _____

sale _____

sail _____

knew _____

new _____

D Write the spelling words that name things you <u>cannot</u> touch.

1. _blew_   2. _hear_   3. _sale_

4. _knew_   5. _here_   6. _new_

Lesson 19 Contractions with -'ll and -'ve

I'll	she'll	I've	we've
you'll	he'll	you've	they've

A Fill in each blank with a spelling word.

1. My sister says ___she'll___ attend summer school.

2. If you tell me a secret, ___I'll___ never repeat it.

3. ___I've___ got a quarter in my pocket.

4. You must be careful, or ___you'll___ hurt yourself.

5. ___They've___ won all their games this year.

6. If ___you've___ never been to the sea, you should go.

7. If a peacock wants to show off, ___he'll___ spread his tail feathers.

8. ___We've___ got five people in our family.

B Circle the letters that are the same in all the spelling words.

I(ve) you(ve) we(ve) they(ve)

C Answer each question.

1. What word does 've stand for? ___have___

2. What word does 'll stand for? ___will___

D Find the missing letters. Then write the word.

1. _s_ _h_ e ' l l ___she'll___

2. _t_ _h_ e _y_ ' v e ___they've___

3. y _o_ _u_ ' _l_ l ___you'll___

Name _____

Lesson 19   Contractions with -'ll and -'ve

DAY 2

I'll	she'll	I've	we've
you'll	he'll	you've	they've

A Match each contraction with its pair of words.

_e_	**1.** she'll	**a.**	they have
_f_	**2.** he'll	**b.**	you will
_b_	**3.** you'll	**c.**	we have
_g_	**4.** I'll	**d.**	I have
_c_	**5.** we've	**e.**	she will
_a_	**6.** they've	**f.**	he will
_d_	**7.** I've	**g.**	I will

B Fill in the boxes with the correct spelling words.

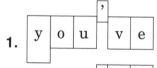

1. y o u ' v e
2. I ' v e
3. I ' l l
4. y o u ' l l
5. s h e ' l l
6. t h e y ' v e

C Use spelling words to complete the puzzle.

Across
1. they have
4. I have
5. she will

Down
2. you have
3. we have
4. I will

¹t	h	e	²y	v	e		
			o				³w
			u		⁴I	v	e
			v		l		v
⁵s	h	e	l	l			e

82

Contractions with -'*ll* and -'*ve*

| I'll | she'll | I've | we've |
| you'll | he'll | you've | they've |

A Find each hidden word from the list. The contractions are written without an (').

life   they've   she'll   wife   we've
you've   strike   you'll   bike

```
s  o  m  e  w  h  e  r  e  o  v  e  r  t  h  y  e
r  w  e  l  l  a  l  i  f  e  i  n  b  o  w  o  w
a  y  u  p  h  i  g  h  t  h  e  r  e  s  a  u  l
a  s  n  d  y  t  h  a  t  i  h  l  e  t  a  v  w
r  h  d  o  f  w  i  f  e  o  l  n  h  c  e  e
i  e  n  a  u  l  u  l  k  a  b  l  y  e  s  o  v
m  l  e  l  l  w  h  e  r  e  o  v  e  y  r  t  e
h  l  e  v  l  r  b  i  k  e  a  i  n  v  b  o  w
s  k  i  e  s  a  r  e  b  l  u  e  a  e  n  d  t
h  e  d  r  e  a  s  t  r  i  k  e  m  s  t  h  a
```

B Use the correct spelling words to complete the story.

Some of us were talking about where ____we've____ taken trips. I told

the group that ____I've____ never been out of the state. Others said

____they've____ only seen one other state besides their own.

"That's hard to believe," said my friend. "You mean ____you've____ never

been out West or seen the Rocky Mountains?"

"No," I told him. "There's so much to see in my own state. I haven't had

time to see anything else."

Name _____

Contractions with -'ll and -'ve

I'll	she'll	I've	we've
you'll	he'll	you've	they've

A Fill in each blank with the correct spelling word.

1. __You'll__ be at school on time, won't you?
   You've   You'll

2. __I've__ never been there before.
   I'll   I've

3. __She'll__ see you in town on Friday.
   She'll   We've

4. I know __he'll__ be glad to see you.
   you've   he'll

5. __I'll__ look both ways before I cross the street again.
   You've   I'll

6. __They've__ been very kind to each other.
   They've   You'll

7. __We've__ always tried to do our best work.
   We've   You'll

8. __You've__ been a joy to teach this year.
   He'll   You've

B Complete each sentence.

1. I've never thought _____.

2. We've always wished _____.

C Write the spelling words in alphabetical order.

1. __he'll__ 2. __I'll__ 3. __I've__ 4. __she'll__

5. __they've__ 6. __we've__ 7. __you'll__ 8. __you've__

Lesson 20

Words with -*shes*

bushes	crushes	brushes	washes
wishes	flashes	dishes	fishes

A Fill in each blank with a spelling word.

1. That camera _____flashes_____ in my face.

2. She _____brushes_____ her hair before she goes to bed.

3. The cat _____washes_____ its paws until they are clean.

4. We planted three _____bushes_____ in our yard.

5. The sign said, "You may have three _____wishes_____."

6. The blender _____crushes_____ ice very well.

7. Is it your turn to wash the _____dishes_____?

8. My uncle _____fishes_____ in the pond on his farm.

B Circle the letters that are the same in all the spelling words.

bu(shes) wi(shes) cru(shes) fla(shes) bru(shes) di(shes) wa(shes) fi(shes)

C Write a spelling word under each picture.

1. _____brushes_____

2. _____dishes_____

3. _____bushes_____

D Write the spelling words in alphabetical order.

1. _____brushes_____   2. _____bushes_____   3. _____crushes_____   4. _____dishes_____

5. _____fishes_____   6. _____flashes_____   7. _____washes_____   8. _____wishes_____

Name _____

Words with -*shes*

bushes	crushes	brushes	washes
wishes	flashes	dishes	fishes

A Put an *X* on the word that is <u>not</u> the same.

1.	bushes	du~~sh~~es	bushes	bushes	bushes
2.	wishes	wishes	wishes	mi~~sh~~es	wishes
3.	crushes	crushes	cnu~~sh~~es	crushes	crushes
4.	flashes	flashes	flashes	flashes	fla~~ch~~es
5.	brushes	brushes	dru~~sh~~es	brushes	brushes
6.	dishes	dishes	bi~~sh~~es	dishes	dishes
7.	washes	ma~~sh~~es	washes	washes	washes
8.	fishes	ti~~sh~~es	fishes	fishes	fishes

B Write each spelling word beside its clue.

crushes	**1.** what a blender does to ice
dishes	**2.** plates, bowls, and cups
flashes	**3.** what the bulb on a camera does
wishes	**4.** hopeful dreams
brushes	**5.** more than one brush
washes	**6.** what a washer does
fishes	**7.** what one does with a rod and reel
bushes	**8.** shrubs or large woody plants

C Write the spelling words that name things you can touch.

1. ___bushes___   2. ___brushes___   3. ___dishes___

Words with -*shes*

bushes	crushes	brushes	washes
wishes	flashes	dishes	fishes

A **Use the correct spelling words to complete the story.**

I know a man who loves to cook, so he opened a small cafe. The cafe is

a few miles out of town. He serves very good food there. But it keeps him

busy all the time.

On his day off, he ____fishes____ for trout to serve at the cafe. He

cleans the fish himself. His wife makes the breads and desserts. She also

helps seat the guests. Their son helps wash the ____dishes____. The oldest

daughter ____washes____ and irons the napkins and tablecloths. Sometimes

she helps serve the food. Much of what they cook is grown in their own garden.

The man says he ____wishes____ he had more free time. "But if I did," he

says, "I'd probably just spend it cooking."

B **Write the simplest form of each spelling word.** *singular*

1. ____bush____ 2. ____crush____ 3. ____brush____ 4. ____wash____

5. ____wish____ 6. ____flash____ 7. ____dish____ 8. ____fish____

C **Fill in the boxes with the correct spelling words.**

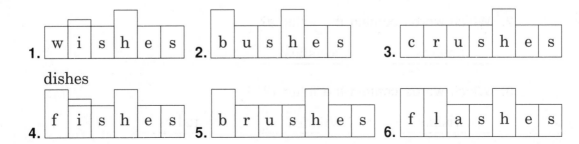

1. | w | i | s | h | e | s |
2. | b | u | s | h | e | s |
3. | c | r | u | s | h | e | s |

dishes
4. | f | i | s | h | e | s |
5. | b | r | u | s | h | e | s |
6. | f | l | a | s | h | e | s |

Name _____

Words with -*shes*

bushes	**crushes**	**brushes**	**washes**
wishes	**flashes**	**dishes**	**fishes**

A **Find the missing letters. Then write the word.**

1. b r _u_ _s_ _h_ _e_ _s_ s   brushes

2. _f_ l _a_ _s_ _h_ _e_ _s_   flashes

3. w i _s_ _h_ _e_ _s_   wishes

B **Use each spelling word in a sentence.**

bushes _____

wishes _____

crushes _____

flashes _____

brushes _____

dishes _____

washes _____

fishes _____

C **Answer the questions with spelling words.**

1. Which words begin with two consonants?

crushes   flashes   brushes

2. Which words contain the letter *a*?

flashes   washes

3. Which words contain the letter *i*?

wishes   dishes   fishes

wrench	wreck	won't	didn't	blew
wring	wrestle	aren't	wasn't	blue
wrist	wren	isn't	hasn't	hear
wrong	wreath	doesn't	weren't	here

A Write a spelling word under each picture.

1. _____wrench_____   2. _____wrist_____   3. _____wren_____

B Fill in each blank with a spelling word.

1. _____Isn't_____ that your mother over there?

2. I called her, but she _____wasn't_____ there.

3. Are your eyes _____blue_____ or brown?

4. The cars went too fast and caused a _____wreck_____.

5. The kittens like to play and _____wrestle_____ with each other.

6. I think I put the _____wrong_____ answer on the test.

7. _____Wring_____ out your swimsuit before you hang it up to dry.

8. I put a _____wreath_____ on my front door.

9. Did you _____hear_____ that loud noise outside?

10. The small flags _____blew_____ in the wind.

11. They will be _____here_____ at two o'clock today.

12. He _____hasn't_____ called me back yet.

Name _____

sale	I'll	I've	bushes	brushes
sail	you'll	you've	wishes	dishes
knew	she'll	we've	crushes	washes
new	he'll	they've	flashes	fishes

C **Write the spelling words that rhyme with the word pair.**

1. rail   tail   _____sail, sale_____

2. few   true   _____new, knew_____

3. wishes   fishes   _____dishes_____

4. clashes   splashes   _____flashes_____

5. dishes   wishes   _____fishes_____

D **Use the correct spelling words to complete the story.**

Our club needed money for new band uniforms. We decided to have a

bake sale. We made about $200 from the sale. Our club leader told us,

" ___You've___ done a good job so far, but the club still needs more money

for the uniforms. ___You'll___ need to make about $500 more." Whew!

It seemed like a lot of money, but we put our heads together to think of other

ways that we could make money. One person from the club said we should

trim ___bushes___ and trees to earn more money. We agreed that this

was a good idea. After we finished trimming, we counted our money. Our

___wishes___ had come true! "___We've___ made enough money to

buy the uniforms!" we said to each other. The leader of our club was very

proud of us.

Words with -*xes*

boxes	fixes	taxes	mixes
foxes	waxes	axes	sixes

A Fill in each blank with a spelling word.

1. My dad ___waxes___ the floor to make it shine.

2. We pay ___taxes___ each year to help support our government.

3. There are many cake ___mixes___ to choose from.

4. Please count by twos and ___sixes___.

5. We piled the ___boxes___ on top of each other.

6. A plumber ___fixes___ stopped-up sinks.

7. Lumberjacks use ___axes___ to cut down trees.

8. The farmer put up a fence to keep the ___foxes___ out.

B Circle the letters that are the same in all the spelling words.

bo(xes)   fo(xes)   fi(xes)   wa(xes)   ta(xes)   a(xes)   mi(xes)   si(xes)

C Write the spelling words in alphabetical order.

1. ___axes___   2. ___boxes___   3. ___fixes___   4. ___foxes___

5. ___mixes___   6. ___sixes___   7. ___taxes___   8. ___waxes___

D Write the spelling words that name things you can touch.

1. ___boxes___   2. ___mixes___   3. ___foxes___

4. ___waxes___   5. ___axes___

Name _____

Lesson 21

Words with *-xes*

boxes	fixes	taxes	mixes
foxes	waxes	axes	sixes

A Write the simplest form of each spelling word.

1. ___box___ 2. ___fix___ 3. ___tax___ 4. ___mix___

5. ___fox___ 6. ___wax___ 7. ___ax___ 8. ___six___

B Use the correct spelling words to complete the story.

I like to go to the dock to watch the ships unload. They bring goods from all parts of the world.

The goods come in ___boxes___. They're unpacked and sold here. But before the boxes can be unloaded, ___taxes___ must be paid on them.

The boxes all have numbers so that no one ___mixes___ them up. I like to imagine what's in the boxes.

C Write a spelling word under each picture.

1. ___axes___ 2. ___sixes___ 3. ___boxes___ 4. ___foxes___

D Find the missing letters. Then write the word.

1. f o _x_ _e_ _s_   ___foxes___

2. a _x_ _e_ _s_   ___axes___

Lesson 21

Words with *-xes*

boxes	fixes	taxes	mixes
foxes	waxes	axes	sixes

A **Find each hidden word from the list.**

boxes	waxes	mixes	spine
foxes	taxes	sixes	ripe
fixes	axes	vine	stripe

```
j  a  c  k  a  s  p  i  n  e  n  d  j  r  i  p  e
m  i  l  l  w  e  n  t  u  p  t  h  w  e  h  i  l
i  l  t  o  f  e  t  c  h  a  p  a  a  i  l  o  f
x  w  a  t  e  b  o  x  e  s  r  j  x  a  c  k  o
e  f  t  a  x  e  s  e  l  l  d  o  e  w  n  a  x
s  n  d  b  r  o  k  e  h  i  s  c  s  r  o  w  e
n  a  n  d  j  f  i  x  e  s  i  l  l  c  a  m  s
e  t  u  m  b  l  i  n  g  a  x  e  s  a  f  t  e
r  t  h  e  n  j  s  t  r  i  p  e  a  c  k  g  o
s  i  x  e  s  t  u  p  a  n  d  h  o  v  i  n  e
```

B **Write each spelling word beside its clue.**

_____fixes_____ **1.** repairs or makes something right

_____axes_____ **2.** tools for chopping wood

_____waxes_____ **3.** polishes for cars and furniture

_____boxes_____ **4.** cardboard containers

_____sixes_____ **5.** numbers

_____foxes_____ **6.** furry-tailed animals

_____mixes_____ **7.** blends together

_____taxes_____ **8.** money we pay the government

Name _____

Lesson 21 — Words with -*xes*

DAY 4

boxes	fixes	taxes	mixes
foxes	waxes	axes	sixes

A Put an *X* on the word that is **not** the same.

1. boxes	do~~x~~es	boxes	boxes	boxes
2. foxes	foxes	foxes	to~~x~~es	foxes
3. fixes	fixes	fi~~z~~es	fixes	fixes
4. waxes	ma~~x~~es	waxes	waxes	waxes
5. taxes	taxes	taxes	fa~~x~~es	taxes
6. axes	axes	axes	axes	o~~x~~es
7. mixes	mixes	mixes	wi~~x~~es	mixes

B Write the spelling words that can either be nouns or verbs.

1. _____boxes_____ 2. _____taxes_____ 3. _____mixes_____

4. _____waxes_____ 5. _____axes_____

C Use spelling words to complete the puzzle.

Across

1. He ____ the floor each week.

4. containers

5. the numbers after the fives

Down

2. chopping tools

3. animals with furry tails

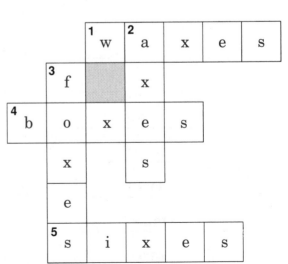

94

Lesson 22 — Words with -*ches*

branches	stitches	churches	crutches
speeches	scratches	catches	matches

A Fill in each blank with a spelling word.

1. The dog ___scratches___ its fur.

2. The outfielder ___catches___ the ball.

3. We will need some ___matches___ to light the fire.

4. The president makes many ___speeches___ each year.

5. The cut on my hand needed ___stitches___.

6. The strong winds broke the tree's ___branches___.

7. He had to use ___crutches___ until his broken leg had mended.

8. I like to visit old ___churches___.

B Circle the letters that are the same in all the spelling words.

bran(ches)   spee(ches)   sti(ches)   scrat(ches)

chur(ches)   cat(ches)   crut(ches)   mat(ches)

C Write a spelling word under each picture.

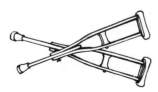

1. ___crutches___   2. ___matches___   3. ___branches___

D Find the missing letters. Then write the word.

1. c _r_ u t _c_ _h_ e s   ___crutches___

2. s t _i_ _t_ _c_ _h_ e s   ___stitches___

Name _____

95

Words with *-ches*

branches	stitches	churches	crutches
speeches	scratches	catches	matches

A Find each hidden word from the list.

branches	scratches	crutches	bite
speeches	churches	matches	drive
stitches	catches	wise	why

```
c  a  t  c  h  e  s  o  s  l  d  k  i  n  g  c  o  s
l  e  w  a  s  a  m  e  c  r  u  t  c  h  e  s  r  p
r  y  o  l  e  s  o  u  r  l  a  n  d  a  m  e  r  e
m  a  t  c  h  e  s  r  a  y  d  r  i  v  e  w  o  e
l  e  s  o  u  l  w  a  t  s  h  e  h  e  c  i  a  c
l  l  e  d  f  o  r  h  c  h  u  r  c  h  e  s  i  h
s  t  i  t  c  h  e  s  h  s  p  i  b  i  t  e  p  e
h  e  c  a  l  l  e  d  e  f  o  r  h  i  s  b  o  s
w  l  a  n  d  h  e  c  s  a  l  w  h  y  l  e  d  f
o  r  b  r  a  n  c  h  e  s  h  i  s  f  i  d  d  l
```

B Write each spelling word beside its clue.

_____branches_____ **1.** the parts of a tree that have leaves

_____stitches_____ **2.** in-and-out movements with a sewing needle

_____catches_____ **3.** what a baseball player does

_____scratches_____ **4.** marks made by a cat's claws

_____speeches_____ **5.** talks given to an audience

_____crutches_____ **6.** used for support if a leg is broken

_____matches_____ **7.** used for starting fires

Words with -ches

branches	stitches	churches	crutches
speeches	scratches	catches	matches

A Put an *X* on the word that is <u>not</u> the same.

1. branches   branches   bre~~n~~ches   branches   branches
2. speeches   speeches   speeches   sque~~e~~ches   speeches
3. stitches   stit~~s~~hes   stitches   stitches   stitches
4. scratches   scratches   scre~~t~~ches   scratches   scratches
5. churches   churches   churches   churches   cha~~r~~ches
6. catches   catches   catches   cot~~c~~hes   catches
7. crutches   cnu~~t~~ches   crutches   crutches   crutches
8. matches   matches   wat~~c~~hes   matches   matches

B Write the spelling words in alphabetical order.

1. branches   2. catches   3. churches   4. crutches
5. matches   6. scratches   7. speeches   8. stitches

C Use the correct spelling words to complete the story.

Every summer my family has a big picnic in the park. I always enjoy visiting

with my cousin, but I will never forget the time we decided to explore the park.

We hiked on the trails and climbed the ___branches___ of a large tree. The

limbs of the trees left red ___scratches___ on our legs. Then when my cousin

climbed down from the tree, she slipped. She cut her leg, but she did not need

___stitches___. That was the last time we went exploring!

Name _____

Words with -*ches*

branches	stitches	churches	crutches
speeches	scratches	catches	matches

A Write the simplest form of each spelling word.

1. __branch__   2. __stitch__   3. __church__   4. __crutch__

5. __speech__   6. __scratch__   7. __catch__   8. __match__

B Match each spelling word with a related word.

__c__ **1.** branches   **a.** doctor

__d__ **2.** speeches   **b.** ball

__a__ **3.** stitches   **c.** tree

__g__ **4.** scratches   **d.** president

__f__ **5.** churches   **e.** broken leg

__b__ **6.** catches   **f.** weddings

__e__ **7.** crutches   **g.** cat

C Use each spelling word in a sentence.

branches _____

speeches _____

stitches _____

scratches _____

churches _____

catches _____

crutches _____

matches _____

DAY 1

Words with *-ies*

pennies	cherries	ponies	cities
babies	berries	puppies	guppies

A Fill in each blank with a spelling word.

1. I have been to several large _____cities_____ .

2. Some _____berries_____ grow on vines.

3. The _____cherries_____ on the tree look ripe to me.

4. Small horses are called _____ponies_____ .

5. _____Guppies_____ are good fish for an aquarium.

6. The dog had five _____puppies_____ .

7. A nursery is where you'll find _____babies_____ .

8. I'll trade you a dime for ten _____pennies_____ .

B Circle the letters that are the same in all the spelling words.

penn(ies) bab(ies) cherr(ies) berr(ies) pon(ies) pupp(ies) cit(ies) gupp(ies)

C Change the plural *ies* in the spelling words to the singular ending *y*. Write the singular words in the blanks.

Plural	Singular
1. pennies	_____penny_____
2. babies	_____baby_____
3. cherries	_____cherry_____
4. berries	_____berry_____
5. ponies	_____pony_____
6. puppies	_____puppy_____
7. cities	_____city_____

Name _____

Words with -ies

pennies	cherries	ponies	cities
babies	berries	puppies	guppies

A Use the correct spelling words to complete the story.

One spring I went to visit my friend. She lives in a small town. I was so excited to visit her because I have always lived in large ____cities____. She said that we were going to a carnival. "What's a carnival?" I thought to myself. I soon found out.

There were games, rides, food, and even animals at the carnival. One of the games I played only cost me ten ____pennies____. My friend and I rode ____ponies____ and ate ice cream sundaes with ____cherries____ on top.

B Write the spelling words that name things you can touch.

1. ____pennies____ 2. ____cherries____ 3. ____ponies____ 4. ____cities____

5. ____babies____ 6. ____berries____ 7. ____puppies____ 8. ____guppies____

C Match each spelling word with a related word.

__b__ **1.** pennies   **a.** horses

__d__ **2.** babies   **b.** coins

__g__ **3.** cherries   **c.** traffic

__f__ **4.** berries   **d.** crib

__a__ **5.** ponies   **e.** water

__h__ **6.** puppies   **f.** vines

__c__ **7.** cities   **g.** pits

__e__ **8.** guppies   **h.** dogs

Lesson 23

Words with *-ies*

pennies	cherries	ponies	cities
babies	berries	puppies	guppies

A Use spelling words to complete the puzzle.

Across

3. small fish

6. big towns

7. very young children

Down

1. baby dogs

2. red fruits with pits

4. cents

5. small horses

Puzzle:

Across:
3. g u p p i e s
6. c i t i e s
7. b a b i e s

Down:
1. p u p p i e s
2. c h e r r i e s
4. p e n n i e s
5. p o n i e s

B Write a spelling word under each picture.

1. cherries

2. puppies

3. pennies

Name _____

Lesson 23

Words with -*ies*

DAY 4

pennies	cherries	ponies	cities
babies	berries	puppies	guppies

A **Fill in the boxes with the correct spelling words.**

1. c i t i e s

2. b e r r i e s

3. puppies
   g u p p i e s

4. b a b i e s

5. p o n i e s

6. p e n n i e s

B **Fill in each blank with a spelling word.**

1. Write three words that can be pets.

   ___ponies___   ___puppies___   ___guppies___

2. Write two words that are fruits.

   ___cherries___   ___berries___

3. Write the only word that contains the letter *a*. ___babies___

4. Write the word that describes a place where people live. ___cities___

5. Write the word for a type of money. ___pennies___

6. Write the word that begins with two consonants. ___cherries___

7. Write the only word that contains the letter *o*. ___ponies___

8. Write the words that have three different vowels.

   ___babies___   ___ponies___

   ___puppies___   ___guppies___

102

Homonyms

hare	tail	sew	heal
hair	tale	sow	heel

A **Fill in each blank with a spelling word.**

1. I had to have a new _____heel_____ put on my shoe.

2. A _____hare_____ is a larger kind of rabbit.

3. Did you ever play "Pin the _____tail_____ on the donkey"?

4. My uncle told me a _____tale_____ about his younger days.

5. We will _____sow_____ the corn seed in the field today.

6. Can you _____sew_____ a button on your shirt?

7. The scratch won't take too long to _____heal_____.

8. I love to feel the wind through my _____hair_____.

B **Circle the correct answer to complete the sentence.**

1. "Sew" and "sow" are not spelled the same, but they _____.

   (sound alike)   mean the same   smell the same

2. The word pairs in this lesson are _____.

   (homonyms)   antonyms   synonyms

3. To "heal" is to _____.

   (cure)   fight   follow

C **Find the missing letters. Then write the word.**

1. t _a_ i _l_   _____tail_____

2. _s_ o _w_   _____sow_____

Name _____

Lesson 24

Homonyms

hare	tail	sew	heal
hair	tale	sow	heel

A **Write the spelling words that rhyme with the word pair.**

1. sail   rail   _____ tail, tale _____

2. know   grow   _____ sew, sow _____

3. feel   meal   _____ heal, heel _____

4. care   dare   _____ hair, hare _____

5. crow   low   _____ sew, sow _____

B **Put an X on the word that is <u>not</u> the same.**

1.	hare	ha~~r~~e	hare	hare	hare
2.	hair	hair	hair	hair	ha~~i~~n
3.	tail	tail	ta~~i~~l	tail	tail
4.	tale	tale	te~~l~~e	tale	tale
5.	sew	sew	sew	s~~o~~w	sew
6.	sow	sow	sow	o~~s~~w	sow
7.	heal	heal	heal	heal	h~~a~~el
8.	heel	heel	heel	b~~e~~el	heel

C **Write a spelling word under each picture.**

1. _____ hair _____   2. _____ heel _____   3. _____ hare _____

104

Homonyms

DAY 3

hare	tail	sew	heal
hair	tale	sow	heel

A Write each spelling word beside its clue.

_____sow_____ **1.** to plant seeds

_____hare_____ **2.** an animal with long ears, a divided upper lip, and long hind legs for leaping

_____heal_____ **3.** to make healthy again

_____heel_____ **4.** the back part of the foot

_____sew_____ **5.** to join by stitches

_____tale_____ **6.** a story

_____tail_____ **7.** the bottom or end part of something

_____hair_____ **8.** fiber or fur

B Write the spelling words that name things you can touch.

1. _____hare_____ **2.** _____hair_____ **3.** _____tail_____ **4.** _____heel_____

C Write the spelling words in alphabetical order.

1. _____hair_____ **2.** _____hare_____ **3.** _____heal_____ **4.** _____heel_____

5. _____sew_____ **6.** _____sow_____ **7.** _____tail_____ **8.** _____tale_____

D Fill in the boxes with the correct spelling words.

1. t a i l

2. sow — s e w

3. heel — h e a l

4. h a r e

5. h a i r

6. t a l e

Name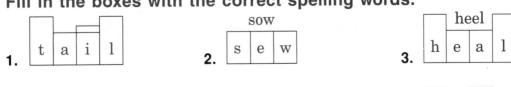

Homonyms

hare	tail	sew	heal
hair	tale	sow	heel

A **Use the correct spelling words to complete the story.**

Once upon a time there was a sly ____hare____. This hare lived on a farm and loved it. He had a nice and cozy hole for a home. He had plenty of vegetables from the fields to eat. His favorite hobby was to play games and make the farmer mad.

One day the farmer spied the hare in the carrot patch. He crept toward the hare and reached out to grab the hare's ____tail____. But the hare hopped away. This made the farmer so mad that he chased the hare across the field. The farmer tripped and fell, tearing his shirt. "You pesky hare!" cried the farmer. "Now I'll have to ____sew____ my shirt back together." But the hare didn't hear the farmer. He was safely back in his hole.

B **Use each spelling word in a sentence.**

hare _____

hair _____

tail _____

tale _____

sew _____

sow _____

heal _____

heel _____

Words with -ves

leaves	knives	shelves	loaves
wolves	calves	thieves	lives

A **Fill in each blank with a spelling word.**

1. The cowboys caught the horse ___thieves___ .

2. Can you help me put the books on the ___shelves___ ?

3. All the ___knives___ in our kitchen are very sharp.

4. Three of our cows had ___calves___ .

5. How many ___loaves___ of bread did you buy at the store?

6. When fall comes, the ___leaves___ always pile up in the yard.

7. Many ___lives___ were saved by the firefighters.

8. ___Wolves___ are not mean animals as some people think.

B **Circle the letters that are the same in all the spelling words.**

lea(ves)   wol(ves)   kni(ves)   cal(ves)   shel(ves)   thie(ves)   loa(ves)   li(ves)

C **Write the singular form of the spelling words.**

1. ___leaf___   2. ___knife___   3. ___shelf___   4. ___loaf___

5. ___wolf___   6. ___calf___   7. ___thief___   8. ___life___

D **Find the missing letters. Then write the word.**

1. _w_ o l _v_ e _s_   ___wolves___

2. _l_ e _a_ _v_ e s   ___leaves___

3. _t_ _h_ i e _v_ e _s_   ___thieves___

4. l _i_ _v_ e _s_   ___lives___

Name _____

DAY 2

Words with *-ves*

leaves	knives	shelves	loaves
wolves	calves	thieves	lives

A **Use the correct spelling words to complete the story.**

Someone who _____leaves_____ his or her home to find a new home is called a settler. Many years ago, the _____lives_____ of most settlers were hard. They had to build their own houses. They grew all their own food.

They also had to protect themselves from _____thieves_____ and bandits. Sometimes they even had to fight off bears and _____wolves_____.

B **Write a spelling word under each picture.**

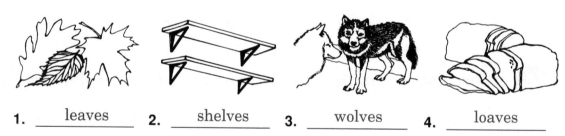

1. _____leaves_____ 2. _____shelves_____ 3. _____wolves_____ 4. _____loaves_____

C **One word is wrong in each sentence. Circle the wrong word. Then fill in the blank with a spelling word that makes sense.**

1. We have to rake (snow) in the fall. _____leaves_____

2. Please put the books on the top (lamps.) _____shelves_____

3. We set the table with forks and (hammers.) _____knives_____

4. We bought ten (quarts) of bread for the picnic. _____loaves_____

5. The (scouts) robbed the bank. _____thieves_____

6. The firefighters saved many (flowers) in the rescue. _____lives_____

Words with *-ves*

leaves	knives	shelves	loaves
wolves	calves	thieves	lives

A Find each hidden word from the list.

leaves	calves	loaves	know
wolves	shelves	lives	pole
knives	thieves	home	stone

```
h  e  y  d  i  d  l  d  l  e  c  d  i  d  l  d  l
e  t  h  s  e  c  e  a  t  a  a  n  d  p  o  l  e
t  w  h  h  e  f  a  i  d  d  l  e  t  h  a  e  c
h  o  m  e  o  w  v  j  u  m  v  p  e  d  v  o  v
e  l  r  l  t  h  e  m  k  o  e  k  o  n  e  t  h
e  v  l  v  i  t  s  t  n  l  s  n  e  d  s  o  g
l  e  a  e  u  g  h  e  o  d  l  i  v  e  s  t  o
s  s  e  s  e  s  u  c  w  h  s  v  p  o  r  t  a
n  d  t  h  i  e  v  e  s  t  h  e  d  i  s  h  r
a  n  a  w  a  y  w  i  t  h  t  s  t  o  n  e  h
```

B Match each spelling word with a related word.

__b__	**1.** leaves	**a.** barn
__e__	**2.** wolves	**b.** rake
__f__	**3.** knives	**c.** steal
__a__	**4.** calves	**d.** bread
__g__	**5.** shelves	**e.** pack
__c__	**6.** thieves	**f.** cut
__d__	**7.** loaves	**g.** books
__h__	**8.** lives	**h.** births

Name _____

Lesson 25

DAY 4

Words with -ves

leaves	knives	shelves	loaves
wolves	calves	thieves	lives

A Fill in the boxes with the correct spelling words.

1. c a l v e s

2. l i v e s

3. t h i e v e s

4. l e a v e s   *loaves*

5. k n i v e s

6. s h e l v e s

B Answer the questions with spelling words.

1. Which words have the long *e* sound?

   _____leaves_____   _____thieves_____

2. Which word has five consonants? _____shelves_____

3. Which words have the letter *o* in them?

   _____wolves_____   _____loaves_____

C Use spelling words to complete the puzzle.

Across

2. They hold books.

4. wild animals

Down

1. robbers

3. Bread comes in ___.

1. t
2. s h e l v e s
3. l
   i   o
   e   a
   v   v
   e   e
4. w o l v e s   s

boxes	taxes	branches	churches	pennies
foxes	axes	speeches	catches	babies
fixes	mixes	stitches	crutches	cherries
waxes	sixes	scratches	matches	berries

A **Write a spelling word under each picture.**

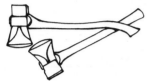  

1. _____axes_____ 2. _____pennies_____ 3. _____babies_____

B **Fill in each blank with a spelling word.**

1. How many cake _____mixes_____ did you buy?

2. I played two _____matches_____ of tennis with my friend.

3. If you break a leg, you may need _____crutches_____ to walk.

4. You'll get _____scratches_____ on your legs if you walk through the bushes.

5. You may need to give _____speeches_____ if you are a leader of a club.

6. I had to pay _____taxes_____ on those packages.

7. How many _____boxes_____ of candy do you have?

8. The cut on his hand will need _____stitches_____.

9. We saw one deer and three _____foxes_____ in the woods.

10. My big brother always cleans and _____waxes_____ his new car.

11. They attend both of those _____churches_____.

12. I put four _____cherries, berries_____ on my hot fudge sundae.

Name _____

ponies	hare	sew	leaves	shelves
puppies	hair	sow	wolves	thieves
cities	tail	heal	knives	loaves
guppies	tale	heel	calves	lives

C **Write the spelling words that rhyme with the word pair.**

1. hives   knives   _lives_
2. fives   lives   _knives_
3. halves   salves   _calves_
4. mow   low   _sew, sow_
5. dare   rare   _hair, hare_
6. sail   pail   _tail, tale_

D **Use the correct spelling words to complete the story.**

My little sister's favorite thing to do is to visit pet stores. I usually take her to a pet store at least once a month. She loves to look at all the animals in their cages on the ___shelves___. After she finishes looking at the animals, she always asks if she can hold the kittens and the ___puppies___. Sometimes I even buy her something from the store.

One time my sister saw some brightly colored ___guppies___ swimming around in a fish tank. She just had to have them! Now they are in a fish tank at our house. My little sister takes very good care of them. Luckily she only wants to keep tame animals as pets. She has never asked to keep ___wolves___ or bears at our house.

DAY 1

Words with *-sses*

dresses	illnesses	glasses	kisses
bosses	classes	guesses	losses

A **Fill in each blank with a spelling word.**

1. Doctors learn how to treat many _____illnesses_____.

2. At school I attend art and reading _____classes_____.

3. I broke my _____glasses_____ and can't see very well.

4. He works for two _____bosses_____ at his job.

5. Her closet is full of new _____dresses_____.

6. Some people greet each other with _____kisses_____ on the cheek.

7. The man at the carnival _____guesses_____ your age.

8. The team had many wins and few _____losses_____.

B **Circle the letters that are the same in all the spelling words.**

dre(sses) bo(sses) illne(sses) cla(sses) gla(sses) gue(sses) ki(sses) lo(sses)

C **Write the singular form of the spelling words.**

1. ___dress___ 2. ___illness___ 3. ___glass___ 4. ___kiss___

5. ___boss___ 6. ___class___ 7. ___guess___ 8. ___loss___

D **Fill in the boxes with the correct spelling words.**

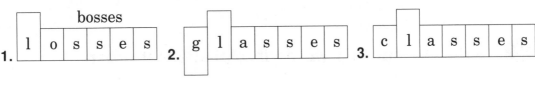

1. bosses l o s s e s
2. g l a s s e s
3. c l a s s e s
4. k i s s e s
5. g u e s s e s
6. d r e s s e s

Name _____

Words with *-sses*

dresses	illnesses	glasses	kisses
bosses	classes	guesses	losses

A Use the correct spelling words to complete the story.

When I was fifteen, we moved from Texas to New York. I was scared my first day of school there. It felt funny not knowing anyone. But the kids in all my _____classes_____ were nice. They asked me where I was from. I told them, "I'll give you three _____guesses_____."

Everyone _____dresses_____ the same in New York as in Texas. They like the same music and play the same sports. I played on a great baseball team in New York. We had almost no _____losses_____.

When we moved back to Texas, I left behind many good friends in New York. I hope to go back there again one day.

B Write a spelling word under each picture.

1. ____glasses____ 2. ____kisses____ 3. ____dresses____ 4. ____glasses____

C Write the spelling words in alphabetical order.

1. ____bosses____ 2. ____classes____ 3. ____dresses____ 4. ____glasses____

5. ____guesses____ 6. ____illnesses____ 7. ____kisses____ 8. ____losses____

Words with -sses

DAY 3

dresses	illnesses	glasses	kisses
bosses	classes	guesses	losses

A **Put an *X* on the word that is not the same.**

1. dresses	dresses	dresses	dresses	tresses
2. bosses	bosses	bosses	dosses	bosses
3. illnesses	illmesses	illnesses	illnesses	illnesses
4. classes	classes	classes	closses	classes
5. glasses	glasses	glasses	glasses	glases
6. guesses	guesses	geusses	guesses	guesses

B **Match each spelling word with the right clue.**

dresses   **1.** puts on clothes

bosses   **2.** leaders or chiefs

glasses   **3.** containers for drinks

illnesses   **4.** sicknesses

losses   **5.** things that are lost

kisses   **6.** belongs with hugs

guesses   **7.** what someone does when they don't know the answer

classes   **8.** places where you learn

C **Find the missing letters. Then write the word.**

1. g l _a_ s _s_ e s   glasses

2. l _o_ s s _e_ _s_   losses

Name _____

Lesson 26

DAY 4

Words with *-sses*

dresses	illnesses	glasses	kisses
bosses	classes	guesses	losses

A Use spelling words to complete the puzzle.

Across

4. sicknesses
5. gets dressed
6. chiefs

Down

1. You get three ___.
2. hugs and ___
3. They help you see better.

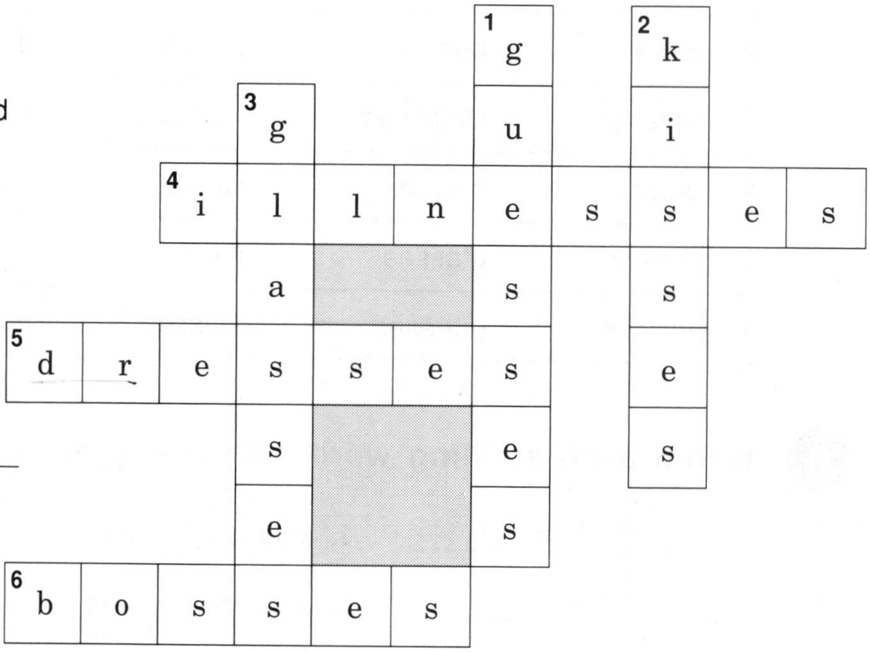

B Use each spelling word in a sentence.

dresses ______________________________

bosses ______________________________

illnesses ______________________________

classes ______________________________

glasses ______________________________

guesses ______________________________

kisses ______________________________

losses ______________________________

Lesson 27

DAY 1

Irregular plural words

men	children	mice	sheep
women	teeth	oxen	geese

A **Fill in each blank with a spelling word.**

1. Cats love to chase ____mice____ .

2. Some farmers use ____oxen____ to pull their plows.

3. My dentist says my ____teeth____ are healthy and clean.

4. ____Geese____ fly in flocks and make honking sounds.

5. The wool for my sweater comes from ____sheep____ .

6. Some games and toys aren't just for ____children____ .

7. Boys grow up to become ____men____ .

8. Girls grow up to become ____women____ .

B **Write the singular form of the spelling words. Use a dictionary for help.**

Plural	Singular		Plural	Singular
1. men	man		5. mice	mouse
2. women	woman		6. oxen	ox
3. children	child		7. sheep	sheep
4. teeth	tooth		8. geese	goose

C **Write the spelling words in alphabetical order.**

1. ____children____   2. ____geese____   3. ____men____   4. ____mice____

5. ____oxen____   6. ____sheep____   7. ____teeth____   8. ____women____

Name _____

Lesson 27

Irregular plural words

men	children	mice	sheep
women	teeth	oxen	geese

A **Write the spelling word that rhymes with the word pair.**

1. hen   ten   men

2. deep   keep   sheep

3. dice   rice   mice

4. piece   lease   geese

B **Write a spelling word under each picture.**

1. geese   2. mice   3. oxen   4. teeth

C **Use the correct spelling words to complete the story.**

My friend is a special kind of doctor. She doesn't take care of grown-ups

and __children__. She treats their pets.

Most of the time she cares for dogs, cats, birds, hamsters, and even

__mice__. She gives them their shots, makes them well when they're

sick, and cleans their __teeth__.

Her partner works with large animals that live on farms. He sees horses,

cattle, and even ducks and __geese__.

I like to visit their office. One time a man came in with a pet raccoon.

Another time someone brought in a pet snake.

Lesson 27   Irregular plural words

men	children	mice	sheep
women	teeth	oxen	geese

A Find each hidden word from the list.

men	teeth	sheep	rose
women	mice	geese	note
children	oxen	slope	drove

```
l   s  h  e  e  p   o  n  d  o  n  b  w  r  i  d  g
e   i  s  f  a  l   l  i  n  g  d  o  o  x  e  n  w
n   g  f  r  o  s  e  a  l  l  i  n  m  e  n  g  d
o   e  w  n  l  o  n  d  s  o  n  t  e  b  r  i  d
g   e  i  s  f  c  h  i  l  d  r  e  n  a  l  l  i
n   s  g  d  o  w  n  m  o  y  f  e  a  i  r  l  a
d   e  y  n  b  u  i  l  p  d  i  t  u  p  w  i  t
h   d  r  o  v  e  w  o  e  o  d  h  a  n  d  c  l
a   y  w  t  o  o  d  a  n  d  c  l  a  y  b  u  i
l   d  i  e  t  u  p  m  i  c  e  w  i  t  h  w  e
```

B Match each spelling word with a related word.

_e_	**1.** men	**a.** cats	
_g_	**2.** women	**b.** wool	
_c_	**3.** children	**c.** kindergarten	
_h_	**4.** teeth	**d.** plows	
_a_	**5.** mice	**e.** boys	
_d_	**6.** oxen	**f.** "honk"	
_b_	**7.** sheep	**g.** girls	
_f_	**8.** geese	**h.** mouth	

Name _____

Irregular plural words

men	children	mice	sheep
women	teeth	oxen	geese

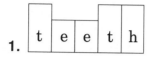

A Fill in the boxes with the correct spelling words.

1. teeth
2. sheep
3. mice
4. geese
5. men
6. children

B Answer each question with a spelling word.

1. Which word has the most letters? children
2. Which word has three *e*'s? geese
3. Which is the shortest word? men

C Use spelling words to complete the puzzle.

Across

4. more than one goose
5. more than one sheep
6. more than one woman

Down

1. more than one tooth
2. more than one man
3. more than one child

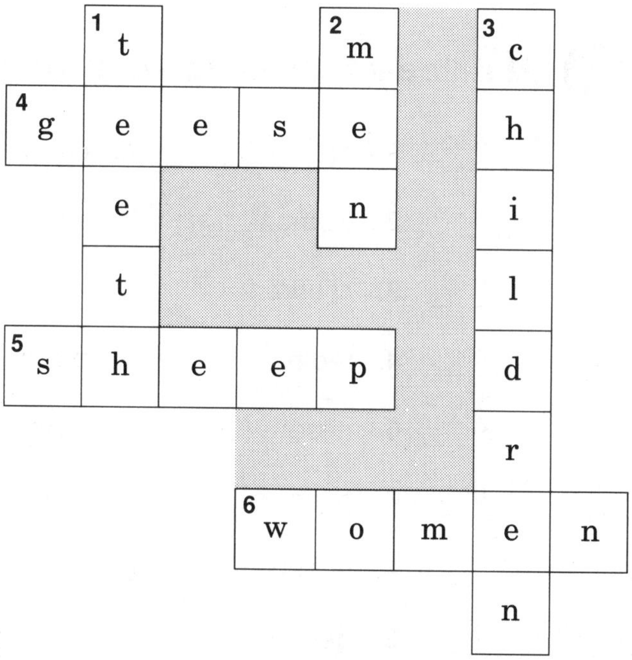

Homonyms

know	write	hour	son
no	right	our	sun

A **Fill in each blank with a spelling word.**

1. Will you ____write____ to me while you're on your trip?

2. We're proud of ____our____ new car.

3. My sister's ____son____ is my nephew.

4. Do you ____know____ how to count change?

5. It takes an ____hour____ to ride the bus home from work.

6. My friend said, "Take a ____right____ turn at the corner."

7. I have ____no____ idea how my pet snake escaped.

8. The ____sun____ is our brightest star.

B **Circle the correct answer to complete the sentence.**

1. "Write" and "right" sound alike, but they _____.

   mean the same   (are not spelled the same)   look the same

2. The words in this lesson are _____.

   antonyms   (homonyms)   synonyms

C **Find the missing letters. Then write the word.**

1. _h_ o u _r_   ____hour____

2. _k_ _n_ o w   ____know____

D **Write the spelling words in alphabetical order.**

1. ____hour____ 2. ____know____ 3. ____no____ 4. ____our____

5. ____right____ 6. ____son____ 7. ____sun____ 8. ____write____

Name _____

121

Homonyms

know	write	hour	son
no	right	our	sun

A Write the spelling words that rhyme with the word pair.

1. ton   fun   son, sun

2. light   sight   write, right

3. flour   tower   hour, our

B Put an *X* on the word that is <u>not</u> the same.

1. know	know	know	kr~~o~~w	know
2. no	~~on~~	no	no	no
3. write	write	w~~r~~ife	write	write
4. right	right	rig~~h~~f	right	right
5. hour	hour	hour	hour	ho~~u~~n
6. our	our	our	o~~u~~n	our

C Match each spelling word with a related word.

_e_	**1.** son	**a.**	moon
_a_	**2.** sun	**b.**	your
_f_	**3.** hour	**c.**	yes
_b_	**4.** our	**d.**	pencil
_g_	**5.** right	**e.**	daughter
_d_	**6.** write	**f.**	minute
_h_	**7.** know	**g.**	left
_c_	**8.** no	**h.**	understand

Lesson 28   Homonyms

know	write	hour	son
no	right	our	sun

A **Use the correct spelling words to complete the story.**

My teacher asked each person in my class to ____write____ a poem. The

poem could be about anything we wanted. But I did not ____know____ what I

wanted to write about. I needed to think about it for a while.

When I went home, I sat down to write my poem. I had so many ideas, but I

couldn't decide which one to choose. "Maybe a walk will help me decide which

idea I like the best," I said to myself. I walked for about an ____hour____.

Finally I thought of something to write about. My poem would be a beautiful

story about the moon and the ____sun____. I couldn't wait to go home and

start writing!

B **Write a spelling word under each picture.**

1. ____sun____ 2. ____hour____ 3. ____son____ 4. ____write____

C **Write the spelling words that name things you <u>cannot</u> touch.**

1. ____know____ 2. ____write____ 3. ____hour____ 4. ____no____

5. ____right____ 6. ____our____ 7. ____sun____

Name _____

Homonyms

know	write	hour	son
no	right	our	sun

A **Fill in the boxes with the correct spelling words.**

1. k n o w

2. w r i t e

3. h o u r

sun, our
4. s o n

5. n o

6. r i g h t

B **Answer the questions with spelling words.**

1. Which words begin with a silent letter?

    _____know_____   _____write_____   _____hour_____

2. Which words contain the letter *u*?

    _____hour_____   _____our_____   _____sun_____

3. Which word contains a silent *gh*? _____right_____

4. Which word is the shortest? _____no_____

5. Which words contain the letter *i*? _____write_____   _____right_____

C **Use each spelling word in a sentence.**

know _____

no _____

write _____

right _____

hour _____

our _____

Compound words with *any-*

anyone	anybody	anyhow	anyway
anything	anyplace	anywhere	anytime

A **Fill in each blank with a spelling word.**

1. There are ___anywhere___ from three to five opossums living under our house.

2. ___Anything___ you can do, I can do, too!

3. I don't know ___anyone, anybody___ by that name.

4. He can come to my house ___anytime___ he wants.

5. What do you want to do that for, ___anyway, anyhow___?

6. You can put the box ___anyplace___ you like.

7. Is there ___anybody, anyone___ here who can open this box?

8. I'm going ___anyhow, anyway___, even if she's not.

B **Circle the letters that are the same in all the spelling words.**

(any)one   (any)thing   (any)body   (any)place   (any)time

C **Circle the correct answer to complete the sentence.**

1. All of the spelling words in this lesson are called _____.

   contractions   compacts   (compounds)

2. All of the spelling words have _____.

   one syllable   (more than one syllable)

D **Find the missing letters. Then write the word.**

1. a n y t _i_ _m_ _e_   ___anytime___

2. a n y w _a_ _y_   ___anyway___

Name _____

Compound words with *any-*

anyone	anybody	anyhow	anyway
anything	anyplace	anywhere	anytime

A Put an *X* on the word that is <u>not</u> the same.

1. anyone	anyone	any~~n~~oe	anyone	anyone
2. anything	anything	anything	anything	any~~t~~hiny
3. anybody	anybody	any~~b~~oby	anybody	anybody
4. anyplace	any~~p~~lace	anyplace	anyplace	anyplace
5. anyhow	anyhow	anyhow	anyhow	any~~h~~ow
6. anywhere	anywhere	any~~w~~heer	anywhere	anywhere
7. anyway	any~~w~~ay	anyway	anyway	anyway
8. anytime	anytime	any~~t~~ime	anytime	anytime

B Write the spelling words in alphabetical order.

1. anybody   2. anyhow   3. anyone   4. anyplace

5. anything   6. anytime   7. anyway   8. anywhere

C Use the correct spelling words to complete the story.

There are times when I can't make up my mind. My friend called and

asked what I wanted to do tonight. "Oh, ___anything___ is fine with me,"

I told him. He asked where I wanted to meet him. "___Anywhere/Anyplace___ you

choose is all right," I said.

"What time shall we meet?" my friend asked.

"___Anytime___ that is good for you," I answered.

Compound words with *any-*

anyone	anybody	anyhow	anyway
anything	anyplace	anywhere	anytime

DAY 3

A Find each hidden word from the list.

anyone	anyplace	anyway	don't
anything	anyhow	anytime	fair
anybody	anywhere	own	chair

```
a  n  y  t  i  m  e  t  h  e  r  e  w  a  s  a  a
n  l  i  t  t  l  e  g  a  n  y  b  o  d  y  i  n
y  r  i  w  h  o  h  a  d  a  l  i  t  t  f  l  y
w  e  a  n  y  o  n  e  c  u  o  w  n  r  a  l  t
a  r  i  g  h  t  i  n  c  h  a  i  r  t  i  h  h
y  e  m  d  i  d  d  l  e  o  f  h  e  r  r  f  i
o  r  e  o  h  e  a  n  y  p  l  a  c  e  a  n  n
w  h  e  n  s  h  e  w  a  s  g  o  o  d  s  h  g
e  w  a  t  s  v  e  r  y  v  e  r  y  g  o  o  d
a  n  y  h  o  w  a  n  d  a  n  y  w  h  e  r  e
```

B Fill in each blank with a spelling word.

1. Write two words about people. ___anyone___   ___anybody___

2. Write two words about places. ___anyplace___   ___anywhere___

3. Write one word about time. ___anytime___

C Match the spelling word with the word that is nearly the same.

___c___ **1.** anybody   **a.** whenever

___a___ **2.** anytime   **b.** whatever

___b___ **3.** anything   **c.** whoever

Name _____

Compound words with *any-*

anyone	anybody	anyhow	anyway
anything	anyplace	anywhere	anytime

A Make as many new words from each spelling word as you can.

1. anyone   =   *any*   *one*   *none*   *an*

2. anything   =   _____   _____   _____   _____

3. anybody   =   _____   _____   _____   _____

4. anyplace   =   _____   _____   _____   _____

5. anyhow   =   _____   _____   _____   _____

6. anywhere   =   _____   _____   _____   _____

7. anyway   =   _____   _____   _____   _____

8. anytime   =   _____   _____   _____   _____

B Use spelling words to complete the puzzle.

Across

2. Can ___ hear me?

3. Is there ___ I can do?

4. anyway

Down

1. anyhow

2. ___ can come to the party.

Puzzle:

1 Down: a n y w a y

2 Across: a n y o n e
2 Down: a n b d y

3 Across: a n y t h i n g

4 Across: a n y h o w

DAY
1

Compound words with *some-*

someone	somebody	somehow	sometime
something	someplace	somewhere	someday

A **Fill in each blank with a spelling word.**

1. _____Somehow_____ he was able to lift the car.

2. I would like to go to town _____sometime_____ today.

3. This sunset is _____something_____ to see!

4. I hope to visit Rome _____someday_____. *(sometime)*

5. Let's go _____someplace_____ and talk. *(somewhere)*

6. Can _____somebody_____ help us? *(someone)*

7. _____Someone_____ is looking for you over there. *(Somebody)*

8. I know that I put my socks _____someplace_____, but I can't find them. *(somewhere)*

B **Circle the letters that are the same in all the spelling words.**

someone   something   somebody   someplace

somehow   somewhere   sometime   someday

C **Circle the correct answer to complete the sentence.**

1. All of the spelling words in this lesson are called _____.

   contractions   (compounds)   compacts

2. All of the spelling words have _____.

   one syllable   (more than one syllable)

D **Find the missing letters. Then write the word.**

s o m e h _o_ _w_   ____somehow____

Name _____

DAY
2

Compound words with *some-*

someone	somebody	somehow	sometime
something	someplace	somewhere	someday

A Put an *X* on the word that is <u>not</u> the same.

1. someone	someone	som~~e~~oue	someone	someone
2. something	something	something	sow~~e~~thing	something
3. somebody	som~~e~~doby	somebody	somebody	somebody
4. someplace	someplace	someplace	someplace	som~~e~~qlace
5. somehow	som~~e~~bow	somehow	somehow	somehow
6. somewhere	somewhere	somewhere	som~~e~~mhere	somewhere
7. sometime	sometime	sow~~e~~time	sometime	sometime
8. someday	someday	someday	someday	som~~e~~bay

B Write the spelling words in alphabetical order.

1. ___somebody___   2. ___someday___   3. ___somehow___

4. ___someone___   5. ___someplace___   6. ___something___

7. ___sometime___   8. ___somewhere___

C Use the correct spelling words to complete the story.

There are those in the world who are ___somehow___ able to write

great songs. One such song is "___Somewhere___ Over the Rainbow."

Writing the words to a song is a lot like writing a poem. But then you

have to add music. It must be a hard thing to do. I think there's

___something___ magic about how a song comes about. Maybe I'll write a

great song ___someday___.

Compound words with *some-*

| someone | somebody | somehow | sometime |
| something | someplace | somewhere | someday |

A Find each hidden word from the list.

someone   someplace   sometime   spare
something   somehow   someday   tear
somebody   somewhere   care   right

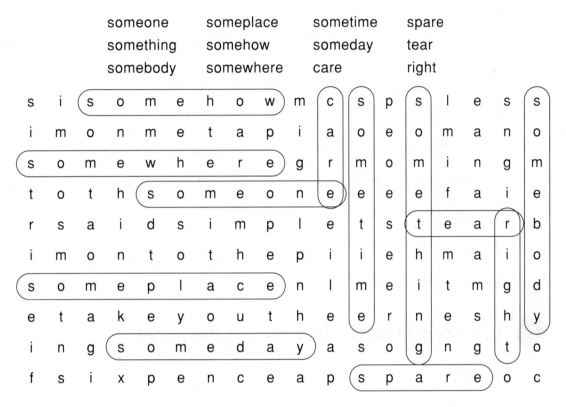

```
s  i  s  o  m  e  h  o  w  m  c  s  p  s  l  e  s  s
i  m  o  n  m  e  t  a  p  i  a  o  e  o  m  a  n  o
s  o  m  e  w  h  e  r  e  g  r  m  o  m  i  n  g  m
t  o  t  h  s  o  m  e  o  n  e  e  e  e  f  a  i  e
r  s  a  i  d  s  i  m  p  l  e  t  s  t  e  a  r  b
i  m  o  n  t  o  t  h  e  p  i  i  e  h  m  a  i  o
s  o  m  e  p  l  a  c  e  n  l  m  e  i  t  m  g  d
e  t  a  k  e  y  o  u  t  h  e  e  r  n  e  s  h  y
i  n  g  s  o  m  e  d  a  y  a  s  o  g  n  g  t  o
f  s  i  x  p  e  n  c  e  a  p  s  p  a  r  e  o  c
```

B Fill in each blank with a spelling word.

1. Write two words about people: ___someone___ ___somebody___

2. Write two words about places: ___somewhere___ ___someplace___

3. Write two words about time: ___sometime___ ___someday___

C Write a spelling word that matches its opposite word.

1. never   ___someday___
                ___sometime___

2. nowhere   ___someplace___
                  ___somewhere___

3. nobody   ___somebody___
                 ___someone___

Name _____

Compound words with *some-*

someone	somebody	somehow	sometime
something	someplace	somewhere	someday

A Make as many new words from each spelling word as you can.

1. someone   = *some   one   me   so*

2. something   = _____ _____ _____ _____

3. somebody   = _____ _____ _____ _____

4. someplace   = _____ _____ _____ _____

5. somehow   = _____ _____ _____ _____

6. somewhere   = _____ _____ _____ _____

7. sometime   = _____ _____ _____ _____

8. someday   = _____ _____ _____ _____

B Use spelling words to complete the puzzle.

Across

1. on a later day

2. someplace

3. Is ___ wrong?

4. somewhere

Down

1. Come see me ___.

2. I'll find a way ___.

Puzzle:

Across 1: `s o m e d a y`
Down 1: `s o ...`
Across 2: `s o m e w h e r e`
Down: `o ... e`
Across 3: `s o m e t h i n g`
Down: `e ... i`
Down: `h ... m`
Across 4: `s o m e p l a c e`
Down: `w`

dresses	somehow	men	mice	know
bosses	anyhow	women	oxen	hour
illnesses	kisses	children	sheep	write
glasses	losses	teeth	geese	right

A **Write a spelling word under each picture.**

1. _____oxen_____   2. _____write_____   3. _____mice_____

B **Fill in each blank with a spelling word.**

1. We saw the _____geese_____ flying over our pond.

2. My grandparents always give me many hugs and _____kisses_____.

3. I'm going to the dentist to have my _____teeth_____ cleaned.

4. I studied hard, and I _____know_____ the answers for the test.

5. The _____children_____ were excited about their new toys.

6. Do you need to turn _____right_____ or left at the light?

7. The _____men_____ and women of our armed forces take care of

   our country.

8. You may need to wear _____glasses_____ if you don't see well.

9. The baseball team had many wins and few _____losses_____.

10. My train leaves in one _____hour_____ and fifteen minutes.

11. Her sister bought two skirts and three _____dresses_____.

Name _____

anyone	no	guesses	someone	anywhere
something	anything	classes	our	somewhere
somebody	anybody	anyway	son	sometime
someplace	anyplace	anytime	sun	someday

C Write the spelling words that rhyme with the word pair.

1. dresses   presses   _____guesses_____

2. go   so   _____no_____

3. passes   glasses   _____classes_____

4. run   bun   _____sun, son_____

D Use the correct spelling words to complete the story.

Has ___someone / somebody___ ever told you ___something___ that was very hard to believe? It happened to my family one time.

My younger brother told us that he had just seen ___someone, somebody___ in the woods wearing a big silver helmet. We thought he had made up the story, so we told him to show us this person. He took us ___somewhere, someplace___ in the woods behind ___our___ house. We looked all around, but we didn't see ___anybody / anyone___.

We waited a minute. Then we saw what he was talking about. The person wearing the silver helmet was the tree trimmer for the electric power company! Everyone in my family started laughing, and we gave my brother a big hug. We felt much better. My little brother really had been telling the truth.

My Word List

Words I Can Spell

Put a ✓ in the box beside each word you spell correctly on your weekly test.

1

- ☐ her
- ☐ fern
- ☐ jerk
- ☐ nerve
- ☐ perch
- ☐ verb
- ☐ herd
- ☐ perk

2

- ☐ turn
- ☐ burn
- ☐ purse
- ☐ nurse
- ☐ burst
- ☐ curve
- ☐ church
- ☐ curb

3

- ☐ launch
- ☐ gauze
- ☐ vault
- ☐ haul
- ☐ fault
- ☐ cause
- ☐ haunt
- ☐ August

4

- ☐ red
- ☐ read
- ☐ not
- ☐ knot
- ☐ maid
- ☐ made
- ☐ be
- ☐ bee

5

- ☐ crawl
- ☐ lawn
- ☐ dawn
- ☐ yawn
- ☐ fawn
- ☐ claw
- ☐ flaw
- ☐ straw

Words To Review

If you miss a word on your test, write it here. Practice it until you can spell it correctly. Then check the box beside the word.

_____

_____

_____

_____

_____

_____

_____

_____

_____

_____

_____

_____

_____

_____

_____

_____

_____

_____

Name _____

Words I Can Spell

Put a ✓ in the box beside each word you spell correctly on your weekly test.

Words To Review

If you miss a word on your test, write it here. Practice it until you can spell it correctly. Then check the box beside the word.

6

- ☐ foot
- ☐ hook
- ☐ wood
- ☐ brook
- ☐ stood
- ☐ hood
- ☐ crook
- ☐ cook

7

- ☐ food
- ☐ noon
- ☐ bloom
- ☐ loose
- ☐ booth
- ☐ tooth
- ☐ goose
- ☐ proof

8

- ☐ thief
- ☐ chief
- ☐ niece
- ☐ piece
- ☐ field
- ☐ shield
- ☐ brief
- ☐ yield

9

- ☐ road
- ☐ rode
- ☐ pail
- ☐ pale
- ☐ ate
- ☐ eight
- ☐ see
- ☐ sea

10

- ☐ breath
- ☐ spread
- ☐ thread
- ☐ ready
- ☐ feather
- ☐ heavy
- ☐ weather
- ☐ leather

Words I Can Spell

Put a ✓ in the box beside each word you spell correctly on your weekly test.

Words To Review

If you miss a word on your test, write it here. Practice it until you can spell it correctly. Then check the box beside the word.

11

- ☐ heard
- ☐ learn
- ☐ earn
- ☐ pearl
- ☐ earth
- ☐ search
- ☐ yearn
- ☐ early

12

- ☐ cry
- ☐ fry
- ☐ dry
- ☐ shy
- ☐ fly
- ☐ sky
- ☐ spy
- ☐ pry

13

- ☐ to
- ☐ two
- ☐ for
- ☐ four
- ☐ bear
- ☐ bare
- ☐ flour
- ☐ flower

14

- ☐ sleigh
- ☐ freight
- ☐ weigh
- ☐ weight
- ☐ neighbor
- ☐ neigh
- ☐ eighty
- ☐ freighter

15

- ☐ kneel
- ☐ knock
- ☐ knife
- ☐ knit
- ☐ knot
- ☐ knob
- ☐ knight
- ☐ knack

Name _____

Words I Can Spell

Put a ✓ in the box beside each word you spell correctly on your weekly test.

16

☐ wrench ☐ wreck

☐ wring ☐ wrestle

☐ wrist ☐ wren

☐ wrong ☐ wreath

17

☐ won't ☐ didn't

☐ aren't ☐ wasn't

☐ isn't ☐ hasn't

☐ doesn't ☐ weren't

18

☐ blew ☐ sale

☐ blue ☐ sail

☐ hear ☐ knew

☐ here ☐ new

19

☐ I'll ☐ I've

☐ you'll ☐ you've

☐ she'll ☐ we've

☐ he'll ☐ they've

20

☐ bushes ☐ brushes

☐ wishes ☐ dishes

☐ crushes ☐ washes

☐ flashes ☐ fishes

Words To Review

If you miss a word on your test, write it here. Practice it until you can spell it correctly. Then check the box beside the word.

My Word List

Words I Can Spell

Put a ✓ in the box beside each word you spell correctly on your weekly test.

21

- ☐ boxes
- ☐ foxes
- ☐ fixes
- ☐ waxes
- ☐ taxes
- ☐ axes
- ☐ mixes
- ☐ sixes

22

- ☐ branches
- ☐ speeches
- ☐ stitches
- ☐ scratches
- ☐ churches
- ☐ catches
- ☐ crutches
- ☐ matches

23

- ☐ pennies
- ☐ babies
- ☐ cherries
- ☐ berries
- ☐ ponies
- ☐ puppies
- ☐ cities
- ☐ guppies

24

- ☐ hare
- ☐ hair
- ☐ tail
- ☐ tale
- ☐ sew
- ☐ sow
- ☐ heal
- ☐ heel

25

- ☐ leaves
- ☐ wolves
- ☐ knives
- ☐ calves
- ☐ shelves
- ☐ thieves
- ☐ loaves
- ☐ lives

Words To Review

If you miss a word on your test, write it here. Practice it until you can spell it correctly. Then check the box beside the word.

_____

_____

_____

_____

_____

_____

_____

_____

_____

_____

_____

_____

_____

_____

_____

_____

_____

_____

Name _____

My Word List

Words I Can Spell

Put a ✓ in the box beside each word you spell correctly on your weekly test.

=== **26** ===

☐ dresses   ☐ glasses

☐ bosses   ☐ guesses

☐ illnesses   ☐ kisses

☐ classes   ☐ losses

=== **27** ===

☐ men   ☐ mice

☐ women   ☐ oxen

☐ children   ☐ sheep

☐ teeth   ☐ geese

=== **28** ===

☐ know   ☐ hour

☐ no   ☐ our

☐ write   ☐ son

☐ right   ☐ sun

=== **29** ===

☐ anyone   ☐ anyhow

☐ anything   ☐ anywhere

☐ anybody   ☐ anyway

☐ anyplace   ☐ anytime

=== **30** ===

☐ someone   ☐ somehow

☐ something   ☐ somewhere

☐ somebody   ☐ sometime

☐ someplace   ☐ someday

Words To Review

If you miss a word on your test, write it here. Practice it until you can spell it correctly. Then check the box beside the word.

Word Study Sheet

(Make a check mark after each step.)

Words	1 Look at the Word	2 Say the Word	3 Think About Each Letter	4 Spell the Word Aloud	5 Write the Word	6 Check the Spelling	7 Repeat Steps (if needed)

Name _____

Graph Your Progress

(Color or shade in the boxes.)

Number of words correctly spelled:

	Lesson 1	Lesson 2	Lesson 3	Lesson 4	Lesson 5	Lesson 6	Lesson 7	Lesson 8	Lesson 9	Lesson 10	Lesson 11	Lesson 12	Lesson 13	Lesson 14	Lesson 15	Lesson 16	Lesson 17	Lesson 18	Lesson 19	Lesson 20	Lesson 21	Lesson 22	Lesson 23	Lesson 24	Lesson 25	Lesson 26	Lesson 27	Lesson 28	Lesson 29	Lesson 30
8																														
7																														
6																														
5																														
4																														
3																														
2																														
1																														

142

Name _____